The Seizure of State Power

Michael Velli

The Seizure of State Power first appeared in 1972 as part of *Manual for Revolutionary Leaders*, published by Black & Red, PO Box 02374, Detroit, Michigan 48202. This edition published in October 1992 by Phoenix Press, PO Box 824, London, N1 9DL. Printed and bound by BPCC Wheatons, Exeter.

0 948984 23 6

The Seizure of State Power

The present century is a period of successful seizures of State power by revolutionary leaders. A substantial part of the world's population is experiencing the social consequences of these successes. These historical successes have created the expectation that careful imitation of the deeds of the successful leaders can lead to similar results. It must be said at the outset that this expectation may be unfounded. It may happen that careful application of similar procedures does not lead to similar results. It may happen that devoted revolutionary organizers fail to realize their goal. Aspiring revolutionary leaders may find themselves *faced with a situation in which almost all of the people whose interests are served by these goals, and who should be, or even are, sympathetic to revolution, neither understand the specific tasks involved in making a revolution nor participate in accomplishing them.*

History does not necessarily absolve all revolutionary leaders who aspire to seize State power. The fact is that the seizure of State power by a revolutionary organization may fail. In the face of the concrete possibility of failure, it becomes necessary for revolutionary leaders to rid themselves of illusions inherited from the past, and to determine with accuracy and care the real conditions for the successful seizure of State power. The assumptions of classical revolutionary theory* must be re-examined in the light of contemporary practice. We must determine whether or not the conditions described by classical revolutionary theory are historically possible, whether or not they are necessary for

*The fact that revolutionary theory is 'classical' is a peculiarity of our age. But this fact is not itself more peculiar than the fact that the main proponents of revolutionary theory are rulers, or the fact that the seizure of State power is the goal of revolutionary organizations, or the fact that leaders, officials, armies and States are revolutionary.

the rise of a revolutionary organization, whether or not they suffice to assure the success of such an organization.

The supreme condition for the seizure of State power by a revolutionary organization—a condition which has come to be regarded as self-evident, as a **sine qua non**—is a revolutionary situation, a revolution. According to classical revolutionary theory, such a situation is not synonymous with the rise to power of a revolutionary organization; such a situation is a precondition for the organization's rise to power. Before examining how such a situation creates the field out of which a revolutionary organization can seize power, we will examine what this situation consists of.

According to the classics, *a revolution, a real, profound, a 'people's' revolution, is the incredibly complicated and painful process of the death of the old and birth of the new social order, of the mode of life of tens of millions of people. It is set in motion by a mighty burst of creative enthusiasm that stems from the people themselves. —The people and the people alone are the moving force, the creators of universal history. —The masses are the real heroes. —The popular masses are endowed with unlimited creative powers. They are able to organize and direct their energy to any and all the branches of human activity. They are able to deal with the task of production over its entire expanse and down to its minutest detail.* According to classical revolutionary theory, *such a revolution can be successfully carried out only if the majority of the population, and primarily the majority of the working people, engage in independent creative work as makers of history,* and for this reason, *the emancipation of the working class must be the act of the working class itself.*

This *independent creative work* on the part of the *creators of universal history* is not the goal or the outcome of a revolutionary situation; according to classical revolutionary theory, this *mighty burst of creative enthusiasm* is the precondition for the seizure of State power by a revolutionary organization; it is the condition without which revolutionary leaders cannot succeed. According to the classics, *no matter how active a group of leaders may be, their activity will amount to nothing more than the sterile efforts of a handful of individuals if it is not related to the activity of the great masses.* This is why the seizure of power by revolutionary leaders *must rely upon a revolutionary upsurge of the people, upon that turning point in the history of the growing revolution when the activity of the advanced ranks of the people is at its height, and when the vacillations in the ranks of the enemy and in the ranks of the weak, half-hearted and irresolute friends of the revolution are strongest.* The *mighty burst of creative enthusiasm that stems from the people themselves* is, according to the classics, a necessary condition for the rise and success of the revolutionary organization—and not only a necessary condition, but an *indestructible wall; the masses, the millions on millions of people who support the revolution with all their heart and all their thought are a wall that no force on earth can ever destroy.* Before examining whether or not a revolutionary situation as depicted by classical revolutionary theory is in fact a sufficient or even a necessary condition for the rise and success of a revolutionary organization, we must first of all ask whether or not such a situation is historically possible.

A revolutionary situation, a situation in which *the majority of the working people engage in independent creative activity,* is a situation of crisis for the dominant social order. The powers of the ruling authorities are *sprung into the air.* These powers are sprung into the air, not by the consciousness of the working people, but by their social practice. People suddenly cease to behave in accordance with the prevailing rules; they become independent and creative. The revolutionary situation consists of independent, creative acts; it consists of individual gestures of rebellion. It is known that the components of a revolutionary situation are historically possible. In fact, individual gestures of rebellion are common, everyday events in any class society. Before pondering the historical possibility of a generalized crisis, a revolutionary situation, it would undoubtedly be useful to scrutinize the individual component of such a situation.

An individual gesture of rebellion may consist of a simple refusal to submit to an abuse. For example, an individual may refuse to be penalized for skipping a day of work without medical or other excuses. If the penalty is reasonable, if it is the normal price paid by an individual who skips a day of work, then the individual refuses to submit to a normal consequence of modern social life. By resisting the penalty, by acting as if she (or he) had the right to skip a day of work, as if she had the right to determine her own work schedule, this individual challenges the legitimacy of the penalizer. By refusing to give up her right to determine her own work schedule, she challenges the right of a foreman, manager or owner to determine her schedule. Since the right to determine work schedules is part of the social power vested in these authorities, the individual's gesture of rebellion challenges the legitimacy of this power. The individual's gesture challenges the legitimacy of the social relations. Since this individual did not explicitly abdicate her right to determine her own work schedule to the authorities who wield this power, her refusal puts in question the origin of their legitimacy. Her refusal exposes a social relation through which the individual's decisions are made by personages to whom the individual never gave the power to make such decisions. The fact that she was born into a social system where the power to make such decisions is lodged in specific social personages does not establish the legitimacy of the power lodged in these personages. This merely raises the further question of why previous generations submitted to these officials. Nor does the fact that others submit to the decisions of the instituted authorities establish the legitimacy of the authorities. Their submission reproduces the power of the authorities; their submission makes it difficult for her to rebel; but their submission does not legitimize the authorities. The simple gesture of this individual even unveils the appearance that the authorities wield those decision-making powers that society's individuals are unable to wield. By skipping a day of work she clearly confirms her ability to decide her own work schedule. In fact, she is unable to decide her own schedule only so long as she submits to the decisions of the authorities. The powers wielded by the authorities are not a response to the individual's powerlessness, but its cause. She is unable to decide because the authorities decide, but the authorities do not decide because is is not able to. Thus, though the individual's gesture of rebellion may be ever so modest and temporary, it consists of a refusal to submit to the dominant social order; it is an *independent* act. This modest act simultaneously exposes the legitimacy of the dominant authorities and the complicity of the submissive individual in reproducing the power of the ruling authorities. The individual gesture of rebellion is not a consciousness or an ideology but rather a practice, a form of social behavior that undermines the dominant form. This independent act might give the individual confidence in her own decision-making powers, but it would not, in and of itself, make her particularly receptive to the services which can be offered by revolutionary organizations and leaders.

An individual gesture of rebellion, even if it challenges the dominant social order in its entirety, cannot in fact move it. The gesture of an individual, no matter how 'radical' or 'revolutionary,' is not *the incredibly complicated and painful process of the death of the old and birth of the new social order, of the mode of life of tens of millions of people.* Furthermore, isolated individual gestures, no matter how numerous, do not constitute the *mighty burst of creative enthusiasm* which, according to classical revolutionary theory, is the necessary condition for the rise of a revolutionary organization.

As a matter of fact, various types of individual rebellious gestures as well as various types of revolutionary organizations coexist with the normal functioning of the dominant social order The coexistence of rebellious gestures with revolutionary organizations, and even the coexistence of both with the dominant social order, does not create a revolutionary situation, nor a revolution, nor the seizure of power by the revolutionary organization.

Individual gestures of rebellion, independent creative acts, may become components of a revolutionary situation. Before determining whether or not they would then constitute a ladder for the rise to power of a revolutionary organization, we must determine the historical possibility of the *mighty burst* of creative activity which can lead to *the death of the old and birth of the new.*

A revolutionary situation consists of a generalization of individual gestures of rebellion. But this does not mean that every generalization of individual gestures constitutes a revolutionary situation. For example, rebellion against parental authority is relatively widespread but does not constitute a revolutionary situation. Such an act can even lead to some kind of independence for an individual, without thereby creating any kind of social crisis. If an individual leaves his parents and moves in with an uncle, he does not become independent of parental authority; he merely subordinates himself to a different wielder of the same authority. But in contemporary circumstances the individual who leaves his parents will probably refrain from moving in with uncles. He will cease to be subject to parental authority. If he is a sole offspring, his act will remove the authority of his parents. He will achieve relative independence. But he does not create a crisis. His act does not remove parental authority from society. He can nevertheless become independent of parental authority because the powers of parents are very restricted; the authority of specific parents is limited to their own offspring. Unlike the powers of Capital and the State, the powers of the parental office cannot be wielded by interchangeable occupants of the office on interchangeable subjects.

The individual who refuses to be penalized for skipping a day of work is in a somewhat different situation. If she is joined by others, if her rebellion becomes widespread, it could lead to some kind of social disturbance. But if she remains isolated, her alternatives will be similar to those of the individual who rebels against his parents. If she continues to skip days of work, she will probably be fired. Her first alternative might be to find work in a plant where attendance regulations are not enforced. Unlike the individual who removed the authority of his parents when he left them, she would not remove the authority of the foreman in the previous plant. Like the individual who moved in with an uncle and thus ceased to be subject to the authority of his parents, she would cease to be subject to the authority of the foreman who had penalized her. She would still be subject to the authority of officials whose powers are identical to those of the official in the first plant, even though the specific wielders of these powers are more lenient in the second plant. She would still be subject to the constraint which initially gave rise to the rebellion. Her second alternative might be to leave the realm of social activity where work schedules are enforced. This is not very easy, or very common, in a society where work schedules are almost universally enforced. But it is not impossible. She might find any number of marginal activities where there are no officials to enforce work schedules. Or, if she is so disposed, she might become an entrepreneur, in which case she would determine her own work schedule as well as that of others. Like the individual who moves away from parents without moving in with uncles, she would achieve relative independence from a specific form of social constraint. But her triumph would be somewhat of a pyrrhic victory. In order to achieve this relative independence, she would have to remove herself from all the social activities in which this constraint is enforced. Her victory would not enlarge the field of social possibilities; it would not even enlarge her own field of possibilities. If we suppose that she had been aware of the other alternatives before she chose to engage her productive energy in the activity which she is now leaving, then her victory is in fact a defeat. She does not gain the right to determine her own work schedule in her chosen field of activity. She abdicates this power to the authorities who wield it. She capitulates.

But if numerous individuals resist the punitive measures of an official, we have a new situation. For example, if numerous individuals in a given workplace simply stopped performing the operations and motions expected of them, they would not necessarily all be fired. Firing would be a likely outcome if the entire group were as replaceable as the individual who refused to comply with the official work schedule. If the group possesses certain experiences or skills, or if there is a shortage of labor, or if scabs are effectively kept out of the workplace, the group would not be easily replaceable; it would be in a situation analogous to that of a sole offspring. Just as the sole offspring can remove the authority of a parent simply by moving out from under it, this group can remove the authority of the official by ceasing to work. But if the group resumes work when the foreman or manager is replaced with a more lenient one, then their action is analogous to that of the individual who moves in with an uncle. The group removes a particular authority but fails to remove the power vested in the office. They merely replace the specific occupant of the office. Their 'victory' does not change the social relations, and their action does not create a revolutionary situation.

If the individuals in a specific workplace resisted, not only a decision of an official, but the powers vested in the office, they would find themselves as frustrated as the isolated individual who tried to appropriate the power to determine her own work schedule. Ruling authorities have been known to grant a great deal when a workplace is occupied, but they have not been known to give away their decision-making powers. Replaceable or not, workers who attempt to appropriate such powers are likely to find themselves in the street.

But the fact that ruling authorities have not given away their decision-making powers does not guarantee their continued possession of those powers. The fact that the underlying population has until today reproduced these powers does not guarantee that the population will continue to do so. There have been occasions, albeit rare, when an underlying population removed the powers of ruling authorities without asking for permission to do so. It has happened that all the individuals of a society have ceased to perform their expected roles, not during a Sunday or holiday when some forms of play are officially allowed, but during a weekday.

It has happened that people occupied the factories, offices, schools, transportation depots, theaters, and at all these workplaces engaged in all imaginable forms of activity except the normal ones. In such cases all normal activity grinds to a halt. Such a situation constitutes a revolutionary situation as defined by classical revolutionary theory. The orders of the ruling authorities are nowhere obeyed. The authorities lose their decision-making powers. *The people, and the people alone* become *the moving force, the creators of universal history.* The power of the ruling authorities is removed and nothing is put in its place. Such a situation presumably constitutes the field out of which a revolutionary organization may seize State power, since according to classical theory *a revolution can be successfully carried out only if the majority of the population, and primarily the majority of the working people, engage in independent creative work as makers of history.*

Revolutionary situations consisting of a complete work stoppage have even taken place in regions where revolutionary organizations have already seized State power. Such instances do not suggest that the revolutionary situation contributes to the revolutionary organization's maintenance of State power. On the contrary, in a situation where play has replaced serious work in the factories, offices, schools and transport depots of a society, it is not immediately apparent that the officials of a ruling revolutionary organization would be spared the embarrassments of suddenly deposed capitalist officials. It seems, rather, that the embarrassment of revolutionary officials whose organization serves the working people would be somewhat greater than that of their capitalist counterparts who do not perform such a service.

For example, let us again examine the case of the foreman or manager who takes punitive measures against an individual who refuses to comply with the official work schedule. In normal times, when others continue to comply with the official work schedule, the manager is able to threaten the individual, fire him, expel him by force if necessary. But in a situation of universal work stoppage, prudence counsels the official not to attempt to wield his normal powers. The manager is likely to know that, even if he succeeded in entering the occupied workplace, and threatened to fire its occupants, he might be informed that he had lost this power. If in anger he tried to physically remove one or another of the occupants from 'his' plant, he would find himself outnumbered. The official would find himself in a situation where his powers are no greater than those of any other single individual in the occupied plant. The fact of having been the plant's manager would no longer magnify this individual's physical endowments. The manager is likely to find himself in the street. Although in normal times such a situation is likely to be unimaginable to most managers, in case it happens it can reasonably be expected that most managers will refrain from entering an occupied workplace, from threatening its occupants, or from attempting to remove them. The commands of a former official, like the commands of a deposed monarch, would not be executed in a situation where none submit to them. An observant official might consider it wise and prudent to pass himself off as merely one of the powerless millions until the return of better days.

If voluntary submission to the ruling authorities ceases to reproduce the normal activity of daily life, then the normal state of affairs might be re-established by means of involuntary submission, namely by force. The deposed officials might spend their waking hours in strategy sessions with the heads of the police and the military.

Before examining the potential efficacy of the forces of law and order in such situations, it would be instructive to see if, prior to the last resort of calling in the armed forces, the revolutionary manager would have more advantageous alternatives than his capitalist counterpart. Let us assume that the first resort of the revolutionary manager is neither to vanish nor to turn directly to the armed forces of the Workers' State. Let us imagine that the manager whose organization officially represents the interests of the working population enters the occupied workplace in order to reason with its occupants. Let us assume that the revolutionary manager is able to enter the occupied workplace, that its occupants do not externally manifest any animosity toward this representative of the working class. We might even imagine that the exchange between the former manager and the former employees is calm and reasonable, that the occupants treat the comrade manager cordially and respectfully.

In this friendly atmosphere, the former manager might begin by reminding the group that the occupation of the plant is an act which breaks the rules and regulations of the plant. One of the occupants could respond, in an equally cordial manner, that the occupants are aware of this fact, but that the rules and regulations mysteriously disappeared on the day of the occupation; they no longer describe the ways people do things; no one's activity corresponds to the rules anymore; furthermore, comrade manager, those rules and regulations are no longer enforceable.

10

Becoming somewhat less cordial, the manager may try to reason with the occupants a second time. In a society where the revolutionary organization of the working class has triumphantly seized State power, he might point out, such an action is not only abnormal; it is perverse. These angry words need not necessarily put an end to the peaceful exchange. Someone may point out, in a perfectly reasonable tone, that during a time when all the individuals in society have stopped work, it is normal for this group to stop work as well; furthermore, in such a situation it would be abnormal and perverse for this group to continue working.

This statement may prove to the manager that the plant's occupants are not willing to listen to reason, and he might lose his composure. He might, for example, threaten to fire them, to deprive them of their relation to the social means of production. But if the revolutionary manager makes such a threat he will find himself on the same slippery path which led his capitalist counterpart to slide out to the street. Yet even this threat need not put an end to the friendly and cordial atmosphere of the meeting. The occupants may in fact pat their former manager on the back and give him three cheers for his courage.

If the embarrassed former manager retains enough composure to be able to reflect about his situation, he might conclude that the occupants refuse to listen to him because of his relatively low status in the State and the Party. They would surely be more reasonable if a much higher official explained the situation to them. For example, the manager's supervisor, the minister or head of the branch of social activity of which this particular plant is a part, would certainly be able to impose his authority. The occupants would of course have no reason to object to the branch head's visit. They might even look forward to it.

The exchange between the branch head and the occupants would undoubtedly be characterized by even greater geniality than the session with the manager. The branch head might, for example, introduce himself as a courageous fighter during the revolutionary war. He will undoubtedly be applauded; he might even be given a standing ovation. He might then be allowed to give a relatively long, uninterrupted speech on the important role 'his' branch plays in the social economy. The occupants would undoubtedly listen with interest, and they might applaud again. The head might then turn to the matter at hand: 'his' branch clearly cannot perform its role in the present situation; all orderly procedures have come to an end; disorder has seized the upper hand; the occupation of the work places is synonymous with chaos and anarchy. Without showing any overt hostility or disrespect for the former branch head, an occupant might explain that since the occupation of the workplaces, people have in general observed a marked decrease in acts of violence; that relations among people do not seem to lack mutual generosity and consideration; that consequently the branch head's conception of general disorder must be based on misinformation, possibly because the branch head's information channels have ceased functioning. As for the chaos and anarchy, another occupant might calmly point out, these words have lost their former sting; if the playful, relaxed and enjoyable atmosphere which has prevailed since the beginning of the occupations constitutes chaos and anarchy, then perhaps the state of affairs depicted by those words is not as terrible as was thought in former days.

While the branch head loosens his tie to unbutton his shirt collar, the manager might give him a "Didn't I tell you?" glance. "Comrade workers," the branch head might continue, "this act is nothing less than sabotage of social activity."

"Comrade Head," a worker might respond, "in a situation when all our fellow workers have stopped carrying on their former activities, would not our resumption of work be an act of sabotage of social activity?"

This response would convince the branch head that the bizarre description given to him by the plant manager is correct: the working people have lost their reason. If this former higher official is physically impressive, he might stand up and take a deep breath before shouting: "I am going to take immediate steps to close down this plant and to send the names of the occupants to the heads of all other branches of social activity. In that case, comrade workers, you will be forced to beg in the streets for morsels of bread."

"But Comrade Head," whispers a worker who sees no need to shout to the former official, "there's no need to take steps to close the plant. It's already closed. In fact, Your whole branch is closed. And it's no longer Your branch. But if you ever did close down a plant so as to punish its workers, would not that be an act of sabotage of social activity?"

This final insult convinces the branch head that only one official in the entire society possesses a stature adequate to the matter at hand. Only one official is authoritative enough to reason with these people: the President of the Republic. Consequently, after briefing the Comrade President, the one-time manager and the former branch head introduce the Head of the Economy, the State and the Army to the assembled occupants of the plant. The working people are of course flattered and honored to be visited by such an important personage.

The President of the Republic goes straight to the point. He does not mince words. "Fellow workers! You are of course aware that this act is illegal. You are breaking the law."

12

These opening words are followed by silence. None of the occupants of the plant have ever spoken publicly or even privately to such a high official. No one had ever heard such a high official contradicted in public. Several occupants appear to be ready to speak, but their lips begin to quiver, then their knees, and they remain silent. Finally one of the occupants decides to make the attempt. "Comrade President," she says to the three officials, "we are not aware that we are breaking the law."

The President, then the Branch Head, and finally the Manager, begin to smile. They are under the impression that in the worker's words reason has at last begun to prevail.

"The law," she continues, her words traveling through a sea of absolute silence, "—the law: that's not long words and sentences written on the pages of heavy books. The law is what people do, how they behave."

The smiles abruptly end.

"When you say we're breaking the law, Comrade President, you must be thinking of the old law, the law that existed before the occupations began. But that law is nothing more than old books now, Comrade President. That's not how people behave now."

As soon as the silence is broken, it becomes evident to all that it is as possible to speak to the President of the Republic as to any other individual.

"Our action was illegal by your former laws," adds another individual, "but your authority was illegitimate."

The one-time manager and the one-time branch head look expectantly at the former President of the Republic, while their supervisor looks anxiously for the nearest exit. With less assurance than the first time, in fact with a noticeable quiver, he says that by not resuming work immediately, the occupants of this plant are raising their interests above the interests of the Revolution, above the interests of Society, "—nay, above the interests of the Working Class."

"But that doesn't stand to reason, Comrade President," one of the occupants insists in a tone that seems to beg the President of the Republic to listen to reason. "How can our work stoppage be against the interests of the working class if the entire working class has stopped work? If we took your advice, Comrade President, if we went back to work, we would be acting against the interests of the working class."

At this suggestion that the former President of the Republic may be opposed to the interests of the working class, the head of all officials becomes visibly agitated. "Don't you know who I am?" he shouts at the speaker. "I am the President of the Workers' State. Do you take me for an idiot?"

The occupants of the plant are visibly embarrassed when suggestions of laughter are distinctly heard because some individuals were unable to contain themselves.

The one-time President appears not to notice the laughter and continues shouting: "By following this perverse path, you are harming no one but yourselves!"

"If that's the case," someone snaps back, "why is it that the Comrade Manager, the Comrade Branch Head, and you, Comrade President, are so upset about our present activity. If we are only harming ourselves, why are you shouting, Comrade President?"

This interpretation of the former President's behavior puts an end to the peaceful exchange. The three officials take stock of their present situation. It suddenly becomes very clear to them that there are numerous working people in the society, whereas there are only a few managers, yet fewer branch heads, and only one President of the Republic. Consequently, there's only one way left to make the population respond to reason. The three authoritative personages move toward the nearest exit. But before leaving, the President of the Republic freezes the plant's occupants with his last words: "Next time I'll talk to you with words that you're going to understand—words which come out of the barrels of guns."

In short, the last resort of the revolutionary officials is similar to that of their capitalist counterparts: the police and the military. But the resort to armed force does not put an end to the matter.

First of all, during a time when the individuals of a society have stopped performing their normal tasks, it is not certain that the armed forces can be completely counted on. It does not take a great deal of imagination to suppose that the individuals who constitute the armed forces will not, in such a period, respond to commands as obediently and unquestioningly as in normal times. It may be that precisely at the moment when the authorities need them most, the forces of law and order will be least reliable.

Secondly, even though the armed forces may during normal times exert extreme violence against the enemies of the ruling authorities, it is not certain that the individuals who compose these armed forces will be as ready to torture and maim people in a situation where the enemies are not isolated individuals but the entire society. After all, neighbors, friends and relatives are now among the outlaws.

Thirdly, historical evidence does not clearly show that a modern army and police are able to subdue a population that is not passive. In a situation where political and military officials are shot at from every window of every house on every street, it is not immediately evident how the officers of the law could reimpose the deposed authorities short of bombing the city from the air. But such bombing could not yield the desired result, since the bombs would fall on the labor force as well as the productive facilities which constitute the basis of the power of the ruling authorities.

Fourthly, even if the military could temporarily establish a hegemony over the population on the basis of its superiority of arms, it is not certain how long they could maintain the superiority of arms if the plants where armaments are designed and produced are among the places occupied by the insurgent population—not to speak of the places which produce the materials needed for the production of weapons.

In short, it is not certain that there really is a last resort for a social order in which a comprehensive revolutionary situation develops.

It has been shown that the generalization of certain types of individual gestures of rebellion may create a revolutionary situation, a thoroughgoing crisis in which the dominant social order may risk complete extinction. But it has not yet been shown whether or not such a situation contains elements which might contribute to the seizure of State power by a revolutionary organization. All that has been shown so far is that, although such a revolutionary situation can easily be imagined, it cannot easily be imagined how such a situation could contribute to the power of a revolutionary organization that has already seized the State apparatus.

Undoubtedly revolutionary organizations that have already seized State power no longer need revolutionary situations. It seems obvious that such organizations can only lose their gains in case a revolutionary situation occurs after their victory. Undoubtedly a far more important question for revolutionary leaders is whether or not a revolutionary situation contributes to the seizure of State power by a revolutionary organization that has not already seized it. In order to explore this question it is necessary to classify revolutionary organizations by type and size, at least crudely, since in normal times capitalist society contains a wide variety of revolutionary organizations, ranging in size and importance from small circles of acquaintances who meet once a month to governmental parties that command the votes of significant portions of a population.

We may begin our examination with the type of revolutionary organization which is best known because it is very influential and is officially designated as a revolutionary organization—an organization that officially represents the working class during normal times. This official representation usually takes the form of a complete monopoly of labor union offices, and frequently the form of representing the working class in the state apparatus itself, for example through possession of the portfolios of one or several ministries and through command of a significant parliamentary minority. In short, such an organization is the official representative of the Labor Movement, the official interpreter of workers' demands, and the official negotiator between the working population and the ruling authorities.

The question is: does a revolutionary situation pave the way to the seizure of State power for a revolutionary organization which has established itself as an official candidate for the offices of the State apparatus, and whose parliamentary and cabinet members have already acquired direct experience in the wielding of State power? Is it self-evident that a universal stoppage of working activity of the type described earlier would pave the way for the seizure of State power by such an organization?

To explore the possibility that a universal work stoppage might end up as a victorious seizure of power by the official representatives of revolution, we might try to imagine what steps a given official of the organization might take in order to secure the organization's revolutionary victory over the striking population.

Let us imagine, for example, that the revolutionary organizer's field of activity is a plant similar in composition to the occupied plant described earlier, except that in this case the plant is located in a capitalist environment where the revolutionary organization has not yet seized State power. Let us suppose that the organizer is already inside the occupied plant; he might, in normal times, have been the union delegate of the workers in the plant.

It is of course to be expected that the plant's official union delegate will use the public address system to speak to the workers assembled in the plant. On the first day of the occupation he might, for example, read congratulatory messages to the workers from the revolutionary cabinet ministers and members of parliament. He also might, on his own initiative, hail the great victory of the working class, its triumph against its class enemy, and its unparalleled courage during the struggle. And finally, he might speak of the great sacrifices the workers of this plant made during the struggle—sacrifices which have undoubtedly exhausted them mentally and physically. Consequently, since the plant's union committee is perfectly able to hold on to the occupied factory and to take care of the necessary business, the tired workers might do well to return to their warm homes and their waiting families until the union committee announces the next general meeting.

The delegate's conclusion will undoubtedly relieve some of the plant's occupants and puzzle others. Those who are relieved may in fact look forward to returning to their homes and families; they may be glad that competent union officials have agreed to take care of the problems of the occupation. Those who are puzzled may also have homes and families, but their desire to leave the plant may not be great enough to overshadow certain suspicions about the delegate's conclusion.

Let us imagine that only one of the plant's occupants finds the words with which to express these suspicions.

"If we go home now," she might ask, "what would happen to our act? The entire population has claimed its rights over everything. If we go home now, wouldn't we be giving those rights away when we've just barely won them? And to whom—to union officials?"

Another occupant might then shout toward the speakers' platform: "Some of us are determined to stay."

Somewhat dismayed, the union delegate might at this point suggest a vote, immediately calling for a show of hands: "Will all those fellow workers who wish to aid the Strike Committee in the administration and coordination of the factory occupation by remaining inside the plant 24 hours a day raise their hands?"

It is to be expected that the formulation of the proposition will create some confusion. But it is conceivable that a few of the occupants will raise their hands, followed by others, until gradually the hands of all the occupants are raised. At that point the union delegate will undoubtedly back away from the microphone to hold a brief strategy session with the other union officials on the speakers' platform, among whom there may be regional delegates as well as a national Party Secretary or a revolutionary member of parliament.

While the union officials confer, one of the plant's occupants might shout to the platform: "Since the plant was occupied by the working people, why do we have to show our identification cards every time we leave or enter the plant?"

This question may prompt the Party Secretary to take the microphone. "The fellow worker has raised a critical problem," the Secretary might explain. "This is the problem of security, the problem of defending the interests of the workers from their class enemies. This is the important function performed by the fellow workers at the factory gates. They are charged with the task of preventing agents of management from entering the plant."

Since it is difficult to make oneself heard without the microphone, those who wish to speak from the floor are forced to shout. This is why the next question someone shouts from the floor sounds like an insult hurled at the Party Secretary: "Are they fellow workers or Party officials?"

Just as the Party Secretary is about to ignore this insult, another individual shouts from the floor: "When did the Party get the right to decide who comes into the plant? Besides, what harm could the managers do now? They no longer even have the power to decide who comes into the plant?"

The group of people on the platform look shocked when yet another individual shouts, "We don't need the Party's police at our gates!"

The officials look at each other as if chaos had broken loose when the occupants of the plant begin to cheer.

Following a long period of enthusiastic cheering, the district delegate calls the meeting to order. She announces that "the first item on the meeting's agenda is the democratic election of a Strike Committee"—but before she is able to propose competent candidates the shouting begins again.

"What on earth for?" shouts an occupant.

"Whose agenda?" shouts another.

The following exchange, consisting of screeching shouts from the floor nearly drowned out by deafening shouts through the loudspeaker, may follow:

MICROPHONE: The function of the Strike Committee is to hold the fort when numbers dwindle, to protect the victories won by the working population.

FLOOR: But we're determined to stay! Unanimously!

MICROPHONE: Furthermore, the Committee has the task of coordinating the strike.

FLOOR: What's that if it's not what we're all doing already? Why should a small group of people do that?

MICROPHONE: It is impossible for all the workers of a plant to negotiate highly technical questions with the plant managers, the owners and the State.

FLOOR: I've got news for you! They've got nothing left to negotiate! Who do you want to negotiate with? The managers don't manage any more, the owners don't own, and as for State officials, they're nowhere to be found! (The shouter is interrupted by laughter and cheering.) Are you going to negotiate with those who are presently occupying the government buildings and the city hall? Haven't you heard that the people occupying those buildings are dancing, playing music and putting on plays?

MICROPHONE: Who will draw up your list of demands?

FLOOR: Who can grant them?

MICROPHONE: What the working people want is—

FLOOR: Who gave you the right to interpret what the people want?

FLOOR: Those days are gone!

FLOOR: When did union officials get a monopoly over the public address system?

FLOOR: . . .

It is not obvious that such a situation creates a "power vacuum" which can be filled by the official revolutionary organization. It is not evident that such a situation would contribute to the seizure of State power by the official interpreters of the population's demands. All that seems evident is that a revolutionary situation of a certain magnitude and momentum would not only re move the powers of the ruling authorities, but also the powers which a revolutionary organization had established in the unions and the government as official representative of the Labor Movement. At first glance it seems that the authority of the official revolutionaries would not carry much more weight in such a situation than the authority of the deposed foremen, managers, owners, branch heads, or the deposed President of the Republic.

Independent creative activity can in fact lead to *the death of the old social order. —A mighty burst of creative enthusiasm,* a revolutionary situation, is a historical possibility. Classical theory assumed that such a situation was the necessary condition for the seizure of power by a revolutionary organization. We have not been able to verify this assumption. On the contrary, we have seen that in the special case of a revolutionary organization which has established positions of power and prestige within the ongoing social order, the key assumption of classical revolutionary theory is false. A revolutionary situation in which *the masses are the real heroes,* in which they *engage in independent creative work as makers of history,* does not provide a fertile field for the growth of an already established revolutionary organization. In fact, the official revolutionary organization is swept away together with the rest of the *old social order.*

However, the fate of an already established revolutionary organization does not destroy the classical assumption that a revolutionary situation is the necessary condition for the growth of a revolutionary organization. Despite the fact that already established revolutionary organizations are the official representatives of revolution, despite the fact that they are almost universally regarded as the spokesmen of revolutionary classes, references to such organizations in classical revolutionary literature are extremely sparse. And the few references that can be found do not in fact treat an already established revolutionary organization as a likely candidate for the seizure of power in a situation where the old social order bursts. On the contrary, such organizations are not considered really revolutionary organizations, but part and parcel of the social order in which they have already established power. Revolutionary leaders who become *officials under capitalism* thereby cease to be really revolutionary leaders. *The functionaries of our political organizations and trade unions are corrupted--or rather tend to be corrupted--by the conditions of capitalism and betray a tendency to become bureaucrats, i.e., privileged persons divorced from the people and standing above the people. That is the essence of bureaucracy.* Furthermore, the positions attained by these revolutionary leaders within the dominant social order are not even considered real steps along the road to the seizure of power, but rather steps away from this path: *Until the capitalists have been expropriated and the bourgeoisie overthrown, even proletarian functionaries will be inevitably 'bureaucratized.'*

Thus despite its public importance, an already established revolutionary organization cannot validly serve as a test case for the classical assumption that a revolutionary situation is the preliminary condition for the rise of a revolutionary organization. Despite the fact that the established revolutionary organization is the official spokesman of revolution and stands ever-ready to seize the bureaucratic-military machine, the sparse explicit references to this type of organization in fact exclude it from the field. It is not with this aim in view that *a mighty burst of creative enthusiasm stems from the people.* The aim of the revolution is not, *as before, to transfer the bureaucratic-military machine from one hand to another, but to smash it.*

A revolutionary situation as described by classical revolutionary theory smashes the dominant social order along with all of its bureaucrats. Before turning to the case of revolutionary leaders who have not become functionaries under capitalism, the case of revolutionary organizations which have not already established power within the dominant social order, we might examine more fully the classical description of the revolutionary situation which is a preliminary condition for the seizure of power by a revolutionary organization. Such a situation *is realized by the initiative of millions, who create a democracy on their own, in their own way. —The old centralized government gives way to the self government of the producers.* This is *the product of the struggle of the producing against the appropriating class, the political form at last discovered under which to work out the economical emancipation of labor.* Furthermore, according to the classics, the working people *know that in order to work out their own emancipation, and along with it that higher form to which present society is irresistibly tending by its own economical agencies, they will have to pass through long struggles, through a series of historic processes, transforming circumstances and men. They have no ideals to realize, but to set free the elements of the new society with which old collapsing bourgeois society itself is pregnant. —In place of the old bourgeois society, with its classes and class antagonisms, we shall have an association in which the free development of each is the condition for the free development of all. —With labor emancipated, every man becomes a working man, and productive labor ceases to be a class attribute. —The political rule of the producer cannot coexist with the perpetuation of his social slavery. —What the bourgeoisie, therefore, produces above all, is its own gravediggers.*

The classical theory of revolution assumes that a social situation which corresponds to the description given above is the preliminary condition for the growth of a revolutionary organization. First of all *the initiative of millions* is a preliminary condition because *all previous historical movements were movements of minorities* whereas *the proletarian movement is the self-conscious, independent movement of the immense majority. The proletariat, the lowest stratum of our present society, cannot stir, cannot raise itself up, without the whole superincumbent strata of official society being sprung into the air.* Without this preliminary condition, the specific project of a revolutionary organization cannot even be considered. *Is it conceivable that such an organization can be created without first abolishing, destroying the state machine created by the bourgeoisie for themselves?* This is not conceivable in classical revolutionary theory; *the precondition of any real people's revolution is the breakup, the shattering of the ready-made state machinery. —Insurrection must rely upon a revolutionary upsurge of the people.* Without such an upsurge on the part of *the great masses,* the activity of *no matter how active a group of leaders would be reduced to the sterile efforts of a handful of people.* As soon as such a *revolutionary upsurge* takes place, the revolutionary leaders *must take power at once--otherwise a wave of real anarchy may become stronger than we are.* And it is assumed by classical revolutionary theory that *the initiative of millions,* the independent creative activity of the producers, also creates the sufficient condition for the revolutionary organization to *take power at once,* namely that an organization which seizes the time and dares to win is bound to succeed: *The entire history of the revolution proves that without the leadership of the working class the revolution fails, and that it succeeds with the leadership of the working class. —The leadership of the working class* means that revolutionary leaders *can and must take state power into their own hands.* Furthermore, classical revolutionary theory even ventures to guarantee that once revolutionary leaders have seized State power, nothing will remove them until they have taken State power over the whole world into their own hands: *Now that the class-conscious workers have built up a party to systematically lay hold of this apparatus and set it in motion with the support of all the working and exploited people--now that these conditions exist, no power on earth can prevent the Bolsheviks, if they do not allow themselves to be scared and if they succeed in taking power, from retaining it until the triumph of the world socialist revolution.*

From the standpoint of revolutionary leaders who today face the possibility of failure, it is critical to re-examine these key assumptions of the classical theory of revolution, because it is this theory and only this theory that *educates the vanguard of the proletariat and makes it capable of assuming power and leading the whole people to socialism, of directing and organizing the new system, of being the teacher, the guide, the leader of all the working and exploited people in organizing their social life without the bourgeoisie and against the bourgeoisie.*

21

Is it certain that a revolutionary organization that has no vested interest in the ruling system, that has not established posts in the Labor Movement or the government, and that cannot lose these established posts as a result of a major crisis, would be able to seize State power out of the revolutionary situation? Or might there be elements in the revolutionary situation which would obstruct the seizure of State power even by such an organization? Is the revolutionary situation a sufficient condition for the rise of such an organization in a case where the former ruling authorities are not restored?

Let us try to imagine militants of such an organization in a revolutionary situation as described by classical theory, a situation *realized by the initiative of millions, who create a democracy on their own, in their own way.* Let us try to imagine if such a situation might contain elements that prevent revolutionary leaders from laying hold of the State apparatus, from setting it in motion, and *from retaining it until the triumph of the world socialist revolution.*

We might follow the activities of such an organization's rank and file militants in a situation where the old regime has definitively collapsed. Streets, schools, railway stations and public buildings are filled with constant motion and with the excitement that the old order has passed and a new day is about to start. For the militants of the revolutionary organization, the revolution has begun. We might try to imagine the feelings of a long-time member of the revolutionary organization as she runs toward a large group of excited people in a crowded railway station. This militant might have been a member of the organization during the dismal days when the majority of the people she spoke to, including her family and her closest non-organization friends, considered her a sectarian, a true believer, even a crackpot. She had nowhere been held in high esteem, or even taken seriously, except by other members of the organization. She had been jailed for addressing crowds at public meetings; the police had raided her apartment searching for radical literature. As she runs toward the group gathered around a newly pasted wallposter, she is in a state of near euphoria as she reflects that all the 'extremist' slogans of former days have become realities.

Former slogans, like 'Let the people decide,' 'The streets belong to the people,' 'Each must make the decisions that affect his or her life,' were the organization's main slogans during the pre-revolutionary period when the population did not have power independent of the ruling authorities. However, slogans which were once appropriate for the banners of the vanguard of the revolution cannot remain the revolutionary order of the day in a situation when these slogans have become facts of daily life. Such slogans cease to be definitions of tasks ahead and become mere descriptions of the status quo. In order not to fall behind the population but to remain ahead, the organization continues to write on its banners orders of the day which point to the tasks of the future. 'Let the people decide' has been replaced by 'The time has come to build the organization of the working class.'

As the militant works her way through the crowd, she listens for statements which might serve as introductions to her presentation of the revolutionary tasks appropriate to the present stage of the struggle. However, the fervor of the discussion and her unfamiliarity with the topics discussed create difficulties for her interruption, and might cause resentment, so she waits and listens and tries to get a notion of the subject at hand.

The group appears to be arguing about the pros and cons of the newly posted proposal on the wall, the subject of which might be, for example, garbage collection. One person argues in favor of collection routes determined by each neighborhood; the next person snaps back in favor of a city-wide network of routes. The group appears to be evenly split. It seems that the issues involved on one side are that a routing system designed by neighborhoods would lead to unnecessarily inefficient routes, while the other side insists that a city-wide network would strain presently available lines of communication. One speaker tries to find a compromise between the two sides by suggesting that each method should be tried, depending on preferences of people in each neighborhood. However, a proponent of city-wide collections immediately snaps back that such a compromise is a victory for the neighborhood collections, since the city-wide network could hardly be efficient if the city trucks had to skirt every

neighborhood that had its own collections. The clear statement of this dilemma causes people to reflect, and the brief interval of silence is the militant's opportunity to bring the attentive and lively group out of what to her seems like a petty frame of reference.

"Comrades," she might say, "the tyrants have been struck down by the might of the working people. The people's victory has begun a new stage of human development. You are discussing garbage, comrades. All the former tyrants have been thrown into the garbage cans of history! This being the case, it is time to begin the next stage of the struggle, it is time for the working class to begin organizing its own activity. Comrades, Organization is the next order of the day. The time has come to write on our banners, 'All power to the people, All power to the Organization of the Working Class.'"

The group applauds enthusiastically, and while applauding they repeat 'All Power to the People, All Power to the Organization!' As she steps away from the wallposter and works her way out of the large circle of people, some individuals pat her on the back, others smile broadly as they shake her hand. But before she has reached the outer circumference of the crowd, people have already resumed the former discussion of city-wide versus neighborhood-wide garbage collections.

Although the militant of the revolutionary organization might be sympathetically received by the group in the railway station, and might even succeed in introducing to these people the slogans which express the revolutionary tasks of the next stage of struggle, from the standpoint of the organization's establishment of a power base the hypothetical scene is inconclusive. Neither the group's sympathy for the militant who in normal times was considered a dangerous extremist, nor their willingness to repeat the militant's slogans, definitively demonstrate that the ground is being laid for the organization's seizure of State power. In fact the hypothetical event suggests that, at least a group of people such as the one described in the station might revert to the problem of organizing garbage collections even after the important problem of the Organization of the Working Class has been clearly communicated to them. Such a

possibility might of course result from the fact that a group of people in a railway station is not in fact a working collective. To see if such an outcome would not be likely in working collectives actually engaged in productive activity, we might try to imagine the organizing efforts of a different militant of the revolutionary organization—say, for example, at a construction site where building activity is actually in progress.

In this illustration we might imagine, not a militant who drops out of the blue into a crowd of strangers, but a militant whose organizing activity is persistent and continuous. He might, for example, return to the construction site every day, and on the occasion when we observe his organizing activity he might already be known by several workers on the site. Let us assume that, in a perfectly friendly spirit, a worker once nicknamed him 'Trotsky' and that those who had come to be acquainted with him greet him with this 'name,' although there are no grounds for assuming that the militant's organization is in fact a Trotskyist organization, or even oriented in that direction.

Let us assume that the fact that only a few of the construction workers are personally acquainted with the militant is not the militant's fault, but is due, for example, to the very same circumstances which might explain why the individuals at this particular workplace might already be engaged in working activity. The militant's limited acquaintance with the individuals on the site might be due to the constantly changing composition of the working collective. Both the changing composition and the fact that productive activity is going on might be due to the peculiar role the construction site played during the height of the insurrection: when the military attacked, all construction sites became sources of materials and equipment for the construction of barricades. Since on numerous occasions the barricades had to be built on the spur of the moment, many individuals who had not been construction workers, many who had not previously even visited a construction site, were forced to learn to use the equipment and the materials in a hurry. Many of the individuals who had mastered these arts during the insurrection

25

continued to frequent the construction sites after the insurrection, no longer to build barricades, but to build new houses, to build accommodations for travelers (the number of travelers would undoubtedly increase astronomically after a complete work stoppage and a successful popular insurrection of the nature described earlier), to build meeting places—in fact, to build all the imaginable places and structures to which individuals have a desire to devote their energies.

This peculiar condition would of course disrupt the militant's organizing efforts. Some of the individuals with whom the militant had good talks and political exchanges may have stayed on the given construction site only for the number of hours or days it took them to master a particular technique or instrument. Others may merely have been travelling through the site, engaging in this particular project merely to become familiar with this realm of social activity, and moving on to other types of activity after their curiosity was satisfied. Yet others may temporarily have joined this particular project and then dropped out of productive activity altogether, either permanently or only for the time being. In short, we have reason to suppose that, of the individuals working at the construction site at any given time, the militant might have the best attendance record.

Let us assume that the militant continues to persevere in his organizing efforts in spite of the shifting composition of the working collective he has been assigned to organize. We might, for example, observe the militant's organizing efforts on the day after a major meeting of the revolutionary organization, a meeting at which the guidelines of the current struggle were defined as moving from the February Revolution, which had established a Dual Power in society, to the October Revolution which would definitively establish the undisputed and uncontested rule of the Working Class. On this particular day, an individual operating the hoist and a person guiding a plank, both of whom are new to this site, seem at once amused and baffled by the militant's reference to February and October, but neither of them stop working.

A construction worker who has just finished putting a steel beam into place from an extremely precarious position on the

scaffolding overhears the comments, warmly greets 'Trotsky,' and climbs down from the scaffolding to relax and wipe the sweat off her forehead. She may already be well acquainted with 'Trotsky' because she is one of the few people who have been working on this site continually since the early days of the insurrection; like others she had learned to use the equipment during the days of the barricades, and after the defeat of the army she and a group of others had stayed at this site to design and build an experimental music hall in place of the office building that had formerly been scheduled to go up. She shakes his hand warmly while looking up toward her beam, and immediately takes up her critique of the revolutionary organization, a critique which the militant has by now heard several times.

"Won't you ever realize, Trotsky, that the play you're acting in ended over half a century ago?"

Part of her technique in ridiculing him comes from her persistence in calling him 'Trotsky,' instead of simply 'comrade' or 'fellow worker,' the designations commonly used in discussions among the militants of the revolutionary organization.

"Can't you learn, Trotsky, that only your 'comrades' are in a play that started in February and ends in October? The rest of the population are writing a different play."

The militant is of course aware of the irony in her tone. But though he knows she is someone who has not learned to take the revolutionary organization seriously, he nevertheless refuses to abandon an opportunity to score good points.

"It's not a question of a spectacle but of the revolutionary practice of the proletariat. There can be no revolutionary practice without theory nor can there be revolutionary theory without practice. The revolutionary theory that corresponds to present conditions is expressed by the slogan: We must move from the February Revolution to the October Revolution. The practice that corresponds to present conditions is expressed by the slogan: We must form Workers' Councils in every mine, every factory, every construction site and every military regiment. These are the *fundamental* tasks of the *actual* political situation."

27

"Bravo!" she says. "But aren't you a few historical moments too late? Now that it's leaked out to people how many and varied their alternatives are, how will you convince them to stay in a given workplace to become a permanent Council? By telling them the old play is about to begin all over again? And how on earth will you convince people to return to military regiments so as to cast them in the familiar role of the Soldiers' Councils? Weren't you there, Trotsky, when half the army disbanded and defected to the armed population behind the barricades, into the houses, and onto the streets from which the remainder of the army was simply overpowered and defeated?"

The revolutionary militant is irritated by the fact that she first of all attributes to him a 'nickname' and then proceeds to attack him by ridiculing the military achievements of his 'nickname.' He nevertheless stands his ground and tries to trip the opponent with another approach.

"Surely you are aware, comrade, that *the highly remarkable feature of our revolution is that it has brought about a dual power. Unless this is understood, we cannot advance.*"

"Why, you must be referring to the power of the population and the power of the Revolutionary Organization, isn't that so Trotsky?" she asks, blinking at the hoist operator who has approached to listen. "And everyone knows, Trotsky," (she seems almost perverse in her persistent abuse of his nickname) "that since only one of the two sides understands the question of Dual Power, the conclusion of the play is already known halfway through the first act."

"*Unless this question is understood,* comrade, *there can be no intelligent participation in the revolution, not to speak of guidance of the revolution!*"

All the individuals on the construction site have stopped working. All eyes are concentrated on the revolutionary militant. This is the first time since his organizing efforts began that he has succeeded in capturing the attention of everyone on the site. He raises his fist and yells, "All Power to the Working Class. All Power to the Workers' Councils!"

The scene at the construction site is at least as inconclusive as the scene in the railway station. Even if we assume that the individuals working at the site are as sympathetic to the organization's slogans as the group in the railway station, the scene does not clarify just how the organizing activity of the revolutionary militant lays the ground for the seizure of State power by the organization. The scene's failure to clarify our question may be due, not to characteristics of the revolutionary organization, but to the assumptions we built into the situation itself. We did not actually prove, we merely assumed, that a productive activity as complex as construction might be possible in the total absence of either the dominant authorities removed from their offices by the work stoppage or a revolutionary organization's seizure of these offices. Such an assumption may of course be illegitimate, since what is assumed is by no means self-evident. In other words, it has not been shown that, in the absence of either a Capitalist Organization at the head of society or a Revolutionary Organization at the head of society, an activity as complex as construction could nevertheless take place. After all, even if we could legitimately assume that individuals on a given construction site might be able to resume productive activity on their own, we cannot go on to assume that everything this implies would also resume 'on its own.' What this would imply is the resumption, in an 'organizational vacuum,' not only of productive activity on an isolated construction site, but also the production and transportation of construction equipment and machinery; the production and delivery of construction materials such as steel, lumber and concrete; the mining and processing of the minerals and raw materials which go into the construction materials. In short, in order to assume the possibility of construction on an isolated site, we are in fact forced to assume the possibility of productive activity in virtually all other realms of social production. This might of course explain why our central question could not be conclusively answered by the scene at the construction site.

Instead of philosophizing abstractly about the impossibility of

29

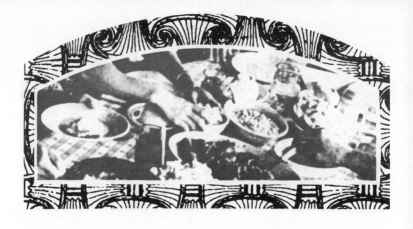

social activity in a situation where society's decision-making authorities have been removed but not replaced, we might enrich our understanding of numerous facets of this question by imagining a revolutionary organizer in yet another social situation. We might, for example, imagine a revolutionary organizer who poses precisely these questions during her lunch break; we might even suppose that this militant takes it for granted that social activity without a decision-making organization is simply impossible (since it is this assumption that accounts for her service and devotion to the revolutionary organization).

In pre-revolutionary days the restaurant where the militant is eating was extremely expensive and catered exclusively to wealthy patrons. At the outbreak of the insurrection it was transformed into a free, self-service neighborhood restaurant. After the battles at the barricades, newly-built neighborhood restaurants were set up on the model of the equipment, cleanliness and quality of meals in this restaurant.

Let us assume that the revolutionary militant, who eats at this restaurant daily because of the superior quality of its meals, never before asked herself about the structure of decision-making in the restaurant itself. She might simply have assumed that the restaurant had an extremely well organized staff, namely a workers' council, as well as a council committee, namely a smaller group who coordinated and organized the well defined tasks of the various staff members. Or she might have assumed that the restaurant's activity had simply continued to be supervised and directed by some of the pre-revolutionary managers and chefs. At any rate, at this particular lunch break she decides to find out which of the two alternatives is actually the case. She decides that, after the meal, she'll enter the kitchen to get a full picture of the restaurant's political structure from the manager or director.

Access to the kitchen is free to anyone. In fact, a poster next to the kitchen door specifically asks guests to visit the kitchen in order to learn one or another of the various arts of food preparation

so as to be somewhat experienced when taking a turn preparing the meals. Of course the militant hadn't ever considered spending numerous valuable hours cooking, since her organizational tasks occupied all her working hours.

Even on this occasion she isn't entering the kitchen in response to the poster asking for volunteer cooks, but to acquaint herself with matters that might be of interest to the Party. She hesitates at the entrance, thinking of the embarrassment she might feel if she were asked to help, but she suppresses this fear and walks up to a man rolling dough. "Could you please tell me who the manager is?"

The man looks at her whimsically, bursts out laughing, and shouts to the others: "Here's another old timer! Can anyone tell her where the manager is?"

A woman sprinkling cheese on frijoles refritos asks the militant, "Is that right, sister? Do you really want me to tell you where the manager is?"

"I'm no old timer," the militant insists. "I'm a member of the revolutionary organization, and I've been a member since long before the revolution. I want to ask some important questions and I'd like to speak to the responsible person, the person in charge."

"Go ahead and ask," says the woman with the cheese. "We can all answer questions. If I don't know the answer someone else may know."

"That's how we do everything here," says a man who is washing dishes.

The militant's face turns crimson and for a moment she considers running out to the street. But she manages to pull herself together. "What I want to know is," she says, turning from one person to another, "I'd like to ask about the organization of this restaurant."

"What about it?" asks the woman.

"Well, for example, when was the workers' council formed, when was the Council Committee elected, how many people are on it—"

"They weren't," says the woman.

"They what?"

"Those things were never formed around here as far as I know," the woman answers.

"What do you mean?"

"Just that," answers a man who is stirring soup. "We've been disabused of all that."

"Do you mean," the militant asks the woman with the cheese, "that the pre-revolutionary organization and staff survived in this restaurant intact?"

"I'll tell you about the pre-revolutionary staff," says the man with the dishes. "They had three people who washed dishes full-time and never did anything else. There were professional vegetable cleaners, a salad staff, soup specialists, two meat cutters, a full time baker, a shipping clerk with an assistant as well as a stock man, five pimps who did nothing but make arrangements, numerous professional bus boys, several staffs of waiters—meat waiters, wine waiters, as well as waiters who only bowed. None of the pre-revolutionary staff have been here since. I suppose none of those people ever want to see a restaurant again."

"Then who coordinates production, who does the planning?"

"You mean what happened to the rest of the pre-revolutionary staff? I can tell you that too. I used to deliver meat here in those days. And I used to peek out to look at the better half. They'd come here to eat in what they called 'their own' restaurant. First of all there was someone they called The Investor. It was said that he passed checks to the others while he ate. One of those he passed money to was a big shot. He was 'In Restaurants' and in lots else besides. A scrawny little man who probably hadn't ever touched dough was 'In Bread.' 'I'm in bread,' he'd say when he shook someone's hand. Another one was 'In Meats and Poultry'—"

"We in the revolutionary organization know about all that," protests the militant.

"No you don't," the man insists. "The one that was 'In Restaurants,' the one they called the Big Boss—he continued to come

around when things started to change. The meals were free and no one raised a fuss about his eating here. He'd always sit all alone, and he'd stay at his table after everyone else had left. It seemed like he didn't want to go back out to the street. Maybe he was afraid that a crowd would start chasing him shouting 'There's that capitalist thief—shoot him!' One night when I was here baking he even came into the kitchen and asked if there might be something he could do. You don't know about all that! You don't know that the man who was 'In Restaurants,' the man who supposedly 'fed thousands of people daily,' the Big Boss as he was called—this man didn't know how to boil an egg! Apparently all he knew was how to send checks to the bank. And when the banks closed down he didn't know anything! I myself told him everyone would be happier if he didn't help in the kitchen, that no one minded his eating here. He continued coming every day when the fighting was still going on, but after the army collapsed he never came back."

The militant is visibly annoyed, and finds that these people are extremely evasive. "Frankly," she says, "I'm not at all interested in the former, capitalist organization of this restaurant. I've studied the social relations and class structure of capitalism to the point where I'm sick of it! What I want to know is how this productive enterprise is organized now—who coordinates the activity, who orders the food, who plans the meals. In other words, how is this place run if not by a Workers' Council guided by a Council Committee?"

"Sister," says the woman, "if one of us can't do it then it just doesn't get done."

"That's no answer!" snaps the militant. "I don't understand your motives for being so hostile to my question, for being so evasive. I'm not so stupid as to believe that a restaurant could function for a day without an **organization**. I happen to know what goes into a loaf of bread! A specific person has to decide how much bread is to be baked so as to know how much flour to order. At the flour mill, in turn, someone is in charge of coordinating the mill's requirements with the agricultural authorities who supply the grain.

33

The same is true of meat and vegetables—not to speak of all the fancy equipment you've got! It all takes coordinators, organizers, planners!"

The baker turns to her and, as if quoting a philosophical text, says slowly: "At the heart of the production process itself, where the productive forces are created, the previous forms of social activity did not exhaust the possibilities of contemporary human existence."

"This is exasperating!" shouts the militant.

"Can you boil an egg?" asks the man stirring soup.

"You're all lying!" she screams. "Productive activity on such a scale simply isn't possible without regular staffs, without coordinators and organizers, without leaders. These tasks can't be left to chance! They're the proper tasks of an organization. For the sake of stability and order the development of the productive forces must be controlled."

"But did you hear of anyone who starved," the woman with the cheese shouts back, "either during the insurrection or after? Did you hear that the food stopped growing because it had lost its managers? Did you hear that all the trucks stopped running until the coming of the organizers? Did you hear that food stopped being distributed because the coordinators hadn't arrived? Did you hear we were all so stupid that we didn't know how to get flour from the mill to the bakery?"

"If all those things are running," shouts the militant, "then it merely proves that there must be Councils and Committees coordinating and directing it."

"And if they aren't," snaps the woman, "we've got to go hungry until the day they do!"

In response to this, the militant storms out of the kitchen. At the street entrance to the restaurant, she turns toward the people who are still at the tables talking. She raises her fist and shouts, angrily, "All Power to the Workers' Councils. All Power to the Council Committees!" No one turns to look at her. People simply continue their conversations.

34

The scene in the restaurant still fails to clarify how a revolutionary situation lays the ground for the seizure of power by the revolutionary organization. In fact, the militant of an organization which was not an established part of the previous social order fares almost as badly as the authorities of the former social order. This may, once again, be due to the assumptions built into the scene, and thus need not alarm aspiring revolutionary leaders. The militants of all the previous scenes were presented as outsiders to the productive activity of the people they were assigned to organize. This assumption of course creates unnecessary obstacles to the successful establishment of power by the organization. If we drop this assumption, if we imagine a militant who is himself involved in the activity of his constituency, might there still be obstacles to the rise of a revolutionary organization capable of seizing power?

We might, for example, imagine an organizer who became personally involved in the productive activity of a printing plant. He might have been assigned to the plant in order to print the organization's newspaper. Such an assignment would have been an extremely important one in the days of chaos and disorganization which immediately followed the success of the insurrection. After the fall of the old order the revolutionary organization would undoubtedly consider it of capital importance to use all the media of communication to implant in the population the slogan 'All Power to the Organization of the Working Class.'

Of course those early days of 'spontaneous' activity and revolutionary euphoria would not be the best time for the organization to find an individual ready to assume such a responsibility. Undoubtedly a large number of members would have been lost to the organization during the insurrection—individuals who took an active part in one or another 'spontaneous' activity and then simply stayed with the group of people with whom they had fought and worked. Let us imagine that the given militant was ready to assume the assignment because, unlike those who ran to take part in one or another 'spontaneous' struggle, he did not abandon himself to the anarchic activities taking place in his immediate vicinity. He waited until the organization developed a clear line, a coherent strategy — and as soon as the line was formulated after the fighting ended,

he was not lost in an anarchic project like so many other former members. He was ready to respond to the organization's call, to assume his responsibilities.

The period immediately after a successful insurrection would also not be the best time for an organizer to assume this particular assignment. This is due to the fact that printing plants, like construction sites and eating places, would have played a specific role during the insurrection itself. A large and once smooth running printing plant might well be in a state of total disarray as a result of a revolution. The organization member might find that there is no responsible person to whom he can give the newspaper articles. Furthermore there is no staff with a clearly defined division of labor to carry out the various steps necessary for printing the paper. The militant cannot easily learn on his own because there are no institutionalized teachers. Even if all the individuals in the plant on a given day considered it extremely important to print the organization's newspaper, there are no established procedures for determining priorities. There aren't even procedures for assigning work. This situation is a direct result of the activity which developed in the printing plant at the time of the barricades. As soon as productive activity ceased to be a source of income, almost all the former wage workers left the plant in mass and never returned. Those who replaced them had in most cases never before seen printing equipment. Since in most cases the newcomers had to disseminate information about an immediate threat, they were forced to learn on their own and in a great hurry. Some learned by leafing through manuals, some buttonholed a one-time printer to show them the essentials, and others were satisfied with barely readable results. Although hardly any of the plant's one-time printers returned after the insurrection, most of the individuals who learned to print during the insurrection returned after the victory with less hurried and more craftsmanly projects, and usually with an intense desire to master the equipment so as to experiment with its numerous possibilities. Although the equipment was probably used to a fuller extent after the insurrection than ever before, the efficiency, order and discipline of the former work force, and also the well defined division of labor, did not return. This situation created nearly insurmountable obstacles for the militant assigned to

36

print the organization's paper.

Thus in addition to having to print the organization's paper, the militant is saddled with the task of having to organize everyone else's activity as well. When the time comes to organize Workers' Councils in every mine, construction site and printing plant, the militant finds himself in a bizarre predicament. He is unable to gather the individuals in the plant on any given day to a meeting. This predicament is largely due to the fact that, although he is in the plant more regularly than anyone else, the unstructured nature of the teaching has prevented him from mastering any of the techniques and arts of printing. This of course affects the general appearance and readability of the organization's newspaper. It also makes it hard for this individual to talk to others about the indispensability of meeting to organize the plant into a Workers' Council. It's not that people oppose such a Council. Only a few respond with comments like, "We don't need that around here." Most individuals simply tell the militant they're too deeply involved in their work and urge him to hold the meeting without them. Since the response of others is generally, "I'll meet whenever the rest meet," the militant is left in the predicament of meeting by himself. To make matters worse, the militant suspects that several individuals think him a poor craftsman with sloppy habits and consider him an obstacle to the activities in the plant.

The first chance to organize a Workers' Council presents itself when a group of people who did not learn to print during the insurrection come to use the plant's equipment. Since the militant is the only one in the plant who regularly receives and welcomes visitors, the new people ask the militant to help them deal with the technical problems. This gives him a pretext for calling the more experienced individuals to a meeting. "There are people here who want to consult you about using this equipment." Thus he succeeds in creating a meeting with the people in the plant on that particular day. The new people also give him a pretext for raising the question of organizing a Workers' Council. "The problems raised by the new comrades cannot be dealt with in the framework of the organizational forms that currently dominate this plant. If this plant is to serve the needs of these comrades and of all the revolutionary peoples, we must all take part

in sharing the responsibilities. Only a Workers' Council provides a structure adequate to such a task."

An individual who has printed multi-color posters since the days of the barricades announces to the new people, "I think no one here has ever turned away anyone who genuinely wanted to observe and learn." After this announcement, she begins to leave the room.

The militant fears he may have let his single chance slip away. "Is anyone opposed to a Workers' Council? Would those opposed raise their hands?"

No one's hand is raised.

"Unanimously approved," says the individual who spoke earlier, leaving the room, visibly annoyed. Others get up and return to their interrupted projects; some pause to ask the new people what specific technique they wanted to learn. Even the new people leave the room and join people engaged in one or another stage of the printing process. The militant is left alone. He succeeded. He puts a large sign outside the main entrance to the plant: "Council of Printing Workers."

The successful formation of the Workers' Council does not in practice improve the militant's situation. In spite of the sign on the door, the membership of the Council varies daily and the Council never meets. The militant continues to print the organization's newspaper all by himself, and since the quality of other people's projects improves as they become increasingly familiar with the techniques and equipment, their attitude to his habits and standards becomes increasingly hostile. Although no one comments on the newspaper's contents, the militant overhears numerous references to its appearance; people seem to consider it a stack of trash paper and an enormous waste of materials. Consequently when the time comes for all productive Workers' Councils to elect delegates to Council Committees, the militant is in a worse predicament than before. In view of the unsatisfactory nature of his success in forming the Workers' Council, he designs a new strategy. He recruits two members of the organization to join him in the plant. Actually numerous organization members wanted to join him when he made a moving speech at the Organization's weekly meeting emphasizing the need to organize at the point of production, describing the low level of consciousness and

apolitical behavior that results from a failure to do this, and calling for people who would represent a revolutionary force in this particular plant. Although he would have liked to return to the plant the following day with numerous comrades, it was decided that all but two of the volunteers should begin similar organizing activity at the point of production in other unorganized plants.

After a critique and self critique of the earlier meeting at which the Workers' Council was formed, the three militants decide not to call for a general meeting to elect the Council Committee. Instead, they take the opportunity of joining a group of individuals who are taking a break and eating. The three militants present the case in favor of electing a Council Committee. No one seems to have a case against such an election. However, one of the individuals eating lunch, a regular user of the printing equipment and an outstanding photographer, says that since most people don't know what such a Committee member is supposed to do, and since he's sure most people wouldn't be willing to devote time and energy to such a Committee, why don't the three proponents of such a Committee simply elect themselves? That wouldn't be democratic, objects one of the militants. Don't worry about that, says the individual; you won't find anyone in the plant who objects to such a procedure. And sure enough, after consulting other individuals who are using one or another instrument that day, the militants find no one opposed to this scheme and consider themselves unanimously elected to the Council Committee.

The three militants become the first regular staff in the plant since pre-revolutionary days. They receive guests, collaborate on the layout and printing of the organization's paper (the quality of which improves somewhat), and they begin to enforce certain minimal regulations, like no-smoking rules. Their enforcement of rules is successful only among newcomers, and then only temporarily; when the newcomers join more experienced persons and learn to execute technical processes on their own, they also learn to disregard even the most minimal rules. However, even the Council Committee doesn't last. The three-member Committee decides that, to acquire the skills needed to teach newcomers and to raise the quality of the newspaper yet higher, the two new militants are to join more experienced

persons to learn halftone techniques and process color printing. In a matter of days both organization members become so involved in the processes of discovery and experimentation that each decides to remain with the work group to which she and he attached themselves. And to make matters worse for the initial militant, both become visibly hostile toward their mentor.

Our militant is again alone, and physically as well as psychologically he can no longer support his assignment. At organization meetings he regularly asks to be replaced, and on several occasions he suggests that the organization print the newspaper in another plant. He even threatens to resign from the organization. However, his resignation is undesirable in view of his service to the organization, and a public admission of his failure is undesirable because it would not serve the organization's image. Consequently, he is promoted. In the light of his earlier election to the Council Committee, namely in the light of his proven popularity among his fellow workers, he is assigned by the organization's leaders to present himself as the plant's candidate for the position of delegate to the Regional Workers' Council.

On this occasion the militant does not attempt to gather even a few individuals in a meeting. He makes it a point to talk to every individual in the plant on a particular day. He is surprised to find that people become very friendly as soon as he mentions that he intends to leave in order to become the plant's delegate to the Regional Council. He takes their friendliness as a sign of approval, namely as a vote. Each individual nods politely as he describes the virtues of the Regional Council: it will determine priorities, coordinate all the activities of the region, allocate resources in the interests of the third world and enforce regional decisions.

Before leaving, the militant prints the slogan 'All Power to the Regional Workers' Council' and posts it on various walls in the plant. A few days after his departure most of these signs are covered by other posters; of the rest all but one are torn down, and on the remaining sign the militant's slogan is scratched out and above it is written a slogan which corresponds to an earlier stage of the organization's struggle: 'All Power to the Workers!'

40

The events in the printing plant are not very probable. Events with similarities to this sequence have occurred, but they've been rare events, unlikely exceptions. Yet if we grant that such events are possible at all, we are forced to draw at least one conclusion. The mere possibility of such a sequence suggests at least one consequence. The conclusion we are forced to draw is that, even in the absence of a restoration of the old order, a revolutionary situation is not a sufficient condition for the development of a revolutionary organization capable of seizing State power.

This conclusion will undoubtedly be a letdown for aspiring revolutionary leaders. But there is no reason why this conclusion should prevent prospective leaders from continuing to try. Our conclusion does not prove that failure is certain, but only that it is possible. Furthermore, the circumstances underlying the imaginary scenes we have drawn suggest that the possibility of failure is very small. First of all a revolutionary situation of the type described is a historical rarity. And secondly, the resumption of productive activity on the part of the population is an even greater rarity: in the light of all previous human history such an event has extremely low probability. Only one tentative conclusion really emerges from the scenes, namely that if such extremely unusual events are possible at all, then a revolutionary organization's seizure of State power will not be the necessary outcome of an extended revolutionary situation.

This conclusion, however limited in scope, makes our central question problematic—namely, just how does a revolutionary situation lay the ground for the seizure of State power by a revolutionary organization? If such a situation does not necessarily lead to such an outcome, then it becomes pointless to ask how it does so. It seems that we've been asking: how does one milk a bull?—or more to the point, how can we get milk out of a beer barrel? Clearly, turning the tap one way or another or even drilling holes of a certain diameter will not yield milk; the only way we'll get milk out of a beer barrel is if we first transform it into a milk barrel. Or, with respect to our question, we should not ask how a revolutionary situation paves the

path for a revolutionary organization; perhaps what we should be asking is: how must a revolutionary organization transform a revolutionary situation in order to seize power out of it. The reformulation of the question makes it clear that in the scenes drawn so far we have been trying to milk a bull.

Once it is clear that it is not the revolutionary situation, namely the population engaged in self-organized productive activity, that lays the ground for the seizure of State power, but that the revolutionary organization must lay this ground, we might proceed to study yet another possibility: are there elements in the revolutionary situation which might prevent the organization from laying this ground? To determine the possibility of such elements, we might imagine that a meeting of the Regional Workers' Council already took place, that this Regional Council consisted of delegates from various Council Committees of printing plants, construction sites, eating places and other productive plants. Due to electoral procedures described earlier, the Regional Council would consist of all the regional members of the revolutionary organization, since the majority of the organization would be there as delegates from plants and the rest as observers. After this meeting the revolutionary organization would no longer be a mere political sect but would represent the population of an entire region; furthermore the organization's members, unlike the militants depicted in the earlier scenes, would no longer be mere individuals with less social authority than that of the smallest customs official at a national frontier. Let us try to determine if an official delegate of such a body might fail to establish the power of the organization among the population.

Let us suppose that a food truck arrives at a garage which was transformed into a neighborhood food distribution center already during the days of the barricades. People from nearby houses gather at the garage and begin unloading baskets and boxes with fruits and vegetables. On this particular day, when the unloading has barely begun, an authoritative voice shouts: "Halt! Stop unloading the truck!"

42

"Who's that dude?" asks a short, heavy man, pointing to a person dressed in a suit and an attaché case.

"Damned if I know," answers the truck driver.

People stop unloading the truck and are hypnotized by the man in the suit, who sets his case on the tailgate of the truck, opens it, and removes a pencil and a clipboard.

"Some kind of survey?" asks the truck driver, a tall woman with a mild voice who glances over the man's shoulder at the clipboard while speaking.

"I am the Regional Delegate for this neighborhood," answers the man in the suit.

"Delegate for what?" asks a woman who is still holding the basket she was unloading.

"Food distribution," answers the delegate.

"You're what?" shouts a man who was passing boxes from the truck.

"I am here to coordinate the distribution of food," says the delegate.

"What's wrong with the way it's being distributed?" asks the truck driver.

"It's in a state of absolute chaos," answers the delegate. "There's no coordination. There are no central records of resources and users. The newly constituted Regional Planning Commission lacks the very data with which to begin bookkeeping."

"But everyone's being fed!" shouts the man on the truck.

"Resources are being irrationally allocated," insists the delegate. "There are constant shortages—"

"You know, that's true," interrupts the woman with the basket. "Last week I wanted strawberries but they were gone by the time I got here."

There is a brief silence. People are apparently thinking of other shortages.

The short heavy man breaks the silence. "Are you and your clipboard going to prevent shortages?"

"The Regional Planning Commission will from now on

determine the output and assortment of agricultural production," answers the delegate, who is trying to read the label on one of the unloaded boxes.

"The people I just got this food from didn't mention any such outfit," says the truck driver, reaching for the box handed to her by the man on the truck.

"I thought the farms were already growing enough to feed the entire population," says the man on the truck, who is reaching for another box.

"There's no plan!" shouts the delegate.

"You mean the plan's going to grow exactly what we want? And no shortages?" asks the short heavy man.

"Your demand in one period will be taken into consideration when the plan for the next period is drafted," explains the regional delegate. He then asks for the size and contents of the first unloaded box, information which he registers on the clipboard when a woman near the box answers. The woman then goes on to ask, "You mean if no one asks for something in the first plan period, then it won't be available in the next period?"

"The plan does not exclude innovation!" shouts the regional delegate, apparently annoyed by a question he considers naive.

"That's very decent," says the man on the truck, with audible sarcasm. "Our alternatives will once again depend on the imaginations of bureaucrats."

The woman holding the basket appears to take a serious interest in the regional delegate. "How would we know what the planners innovated, say for today's meals?" she asks.

The delegate smiles for the first time. "A newsletter will describe the nature and use of new products, and the new items will appear on your weekly order forms."

"Of course!" shouts the sarcastic skeptic on the truck, putting his index finger on his temple.

"What if I don't pick up your newsletter?" asks the short heavy man.

"It will be regularly included with your weekly allotment of food," explains the delegate.

"What else will this newsletter describe?" asks the skeptic.

"It will deal with general political, educational and cultural questions, and it will list politically relevant events, speakers and meetings."

"Wow!" shouts the skeptic. "Now what happens if, for example, I develop some kind of persecution complex; if the notion grows on me that I'm being brainwashed; and if I refuse to have your political propaganda in the same bag with my food?"

"Neighbor, if you don't want the newsletter," explains the woman with the basket, who had missed out on strawberries last week, "if you don't want the newsletter, I guess you won't get the food."

There is general amusement, but people stop laughing when they see the woman with the basket is not smiling. The regional delegate continues to grin.

"Is that right?" shouts the skeptic on the truck to the woman with the basket. "If I don't want the political line I don't eat?"

There is general uneasiness. The short heavy man tries to find a universally satisfactory solution: "Perhaps the newsletter needn't be put into the bags. It could just as well be left on a table, and only those who like it would take a copy."

There seems to be general agreement with this suggestion, and people begin to relax again. But the calm is definitively broken by the mild voice of the truck driver.

"Have we all gone crazy?" she asks. "We've just recently rid ourselves of an incredibly powerful class of rulers. We've just recently started to learn to make our own decisions. And are we already deciding we're going to take orders from the first person who tells us he's our new king?"

The people gather around the truck driver and seem to wake up from a dream. They move toward the back of the truck, form the usual relay line and resume the process of passing boxes and baskets

from the truck to the tables.

The regional delegate's grin is gone. He hurriedly packs the clipboard and pen in the attaché case and, waving the case in the air, he shouts, "In the name of the Regional Workers' Council, I order you to stop!"

"Get out of the way, Mac; save your rap for later," says a large man who bumps the delegate with a box.

"Do you have a regional police to enforce your orders?" asks the skeptic.

People continue unloading. The delegate attempts to block the relay line. He begins to shout, "In the name of all the victories scored by the workers' revolution—"

He is interrupted by two hefty fellows who lift him into the air and begin carrying him on their shoulders.

"All Power to the Workers!" taunts the skeptic, raising his fist.

"All Power to the Workers!" shout several of the people unloading the truck.

"You're all counter-revolutionaries!" shouts the delegate, turning his head toward the people on the relay line. "You'll pay for this!" he threatens, while his carriers increase the distance between the delegate and the garage. "Next time you won't get a mere delegate from a Regional Council," the delegate continues, by now shouting at passers-by in the street, who probably interpret the event as an instance of street theater, or perhaps as a political demonstration. "The next delegate will be appointed directly by the Central Committee of the Council of All Workers' Councils. He'll teach you a lesson in revolutionary discipline!" he shouts to a woman pushing a baby carriage across the street. "Behind the next delegate will stand the might of the armed population!" he shouts to a group of young people picknicking on a lawn. "I'll return to see if you'll scoff into the guns of the People's Army!" He continues shouting threats to all passers-by, frequently raising his fist and repeating, "All Power to the Central Committee of the Council of All Workers' Councils"—until his bearers reach their destination, the seat of the new government, the steps of the National Theater.

The embarrassing predicament of the Regional Delegate, perhaps possible but hardly plausible in any presently known historical circumstances, nevertheless points toward two tentative conclusions: a revolutionary situation such as the one described is not necessarily the most fertile field for the development of revolutionary leadership, and such a situation may contain elements which might prevent a revolutionary organization from transforming the situation into one suitable for the seizure of State power. It not only appears that the situation fails to thrust power on the organization's leaders, but also that it prevents leaders from taking power. However, before regarding these conclusions as final, we might pause to examine yet another possibility. Perhaps the circumstances underlying all the hypothetical scenes presented until now unduly exaggerate the elements unfavorable to revolutionary leadership, while at the same time placing members of the revolutionary organization at particularly poor vantage points from which to realize their goal. After all, every one of the scenes depicts militants who are completely divorced from the new productive activities as well as the experimental social relations developed by the self-organized population, militants who are not only pathetically behind the times but also alien to the liberating spirit of the new social activities, militants who are almost, in a sense, reactionaries. The prominence of such circumstances in the hypothetical scenes would of course exaggerate the likelihood that a revolutionary militant might not succeed. Since such circumstances bias all the earlier scenes, we cannot as yet draw the conclusion that there is nothing at all about self-organized and independent activity that lays the ground for the success of a revolutionary organization. Nor can we as yet conclude that as soon as self-organized activity takes root among a population it will prevent the successful seizure of power by a revolutionary organization.

Therefore, before concluding that self-organized and independent creative activity is not a sufficient condition for a revolutionary organization's success but rather for its failure, we would do well to push our question yet further. We would do well to construct a

hypothetical scene which, unlike the earlier scenes, contains elements which from the very beginning of the insurrection provide a fertile field for the success of the revolutionary organization. We could start by building numerous circumstances favorable to the revolutionary organization and its members into the very structure of the scene.

We might structure the scene around a large electronics plant which, from the standpoint of the revolutionary organization, was in the vanguard of the struggle from the earliest days of the insurrection. Let us suppose that on the first day of the general strike the assembled workers of this plant took decisions which corresponded, down to the last letter, to the organization's definition of the most urgent tasks of the day. For example, after deciding to put the plant's technology at the service of all striking workers, the assembled electronics workers formed a Workers' Council and democratically elected a Council Committee as well as a President of the Council Committee. Let us further suppose that the President of the Council Committee, unlike the militants described in earlier scenes, is not a professional organizer unfamiliar with the technical processes of the plant; on the contrary, she is a worker who had been employed in the electronics plant and had been a member of the revolutionary organization long before the popular uprising. And let us furthermore suppose that the general elections of the Council Committee as well as the election of the President lived up to all the criteria of fully democratic elections. First of all, everyone in the plant voted. And secondly, the criteria on the basis of which candidates were proposed were identical to criteria which are used to select a specific group of people to execute a particular task; for example, when the general assembly selected a team of researchers to develop a communications technology appropriate to the needs of the workers assembled in the plant, the individuals were selected on the basis of their knowledge and experience in this particular area. The same criteria were applied in the election of the Council Committee and the President; the fact is that members of the revolutionary organization were the only individuals among the assembled workers who had both the

knowledge and the experience required for performing the roles of President and Council Committee member.

Under the leadership of its revolutionary Council Committee, and guided by its President, the electronics plant put its entire labor force and all its technology at the service of the revolutionary struggle on the barricades and in the streets. Two-way walkie-talkies were freely distributed to the population; these devices helped coordinate the struggles at different barricades, and enabled reinforcements to come to the rescue of isolated neighborhoods. All the plant's workers personally participated in various struggles, and most of them returned to the plant in order to design and produce two-way radio sets, 'barricade television' sets, and other electronic devices particularly suitable to the conditions of the popular insurrection. Furthermore, the Committee, and the plant's President as well, encouraged people who had not previously worked in the plant to participate directly in the production of devices which responded to their own or their neighbors' specific needs.

The social relations which developed in the plant during the insurrection, with the encouragement and support of the plant's revolutionary leadership, continued to develop after the downfall of the old order. Individuals inside the plant continued to participate personally in the 'outside' projects for which they designed and built electronic devices, and people engaged primarily in 'outside' projects continued to participate in the parts of their projects which took place inside the electronics plant. Thus the plant's workers themselves took part in activities related to food distribution, production and delivery of raw materials, and even motion pictures, while individuals engaged in any number of productive activities were continually attracted by the possibilities of the technology available in the electronics plant, and continually came to the plant to design and build experimental devices. The plant's boundaries, the line between the plant's 'labor force' and the 'outside world,' became unclear.

49

However, the electronics plant which was in the vanguard during the insurrection not only because of the establishment of progressive relations inside the plant itself, but also because of the spread of these revolutionary relations to the entire society, begins to run into some problems. When the time comes for all Workers' Councils to elect delegates to the Regional Workers' Council, the plant's President finds herself in a peculiar dilemma. The Workers' Council which had so creatively responded to the needs of the population during the height of the struggle has not actually met since the general assembly meeting where it was formed. The individuals who now compose the plant's work groups are not the ones who composed the plant's labor force when the Council was formed. Matters which require decision, administration and coordination are not determined by the Council Committee but are informally arranged by the work groups through personal relations between suppliers, producers and users. What's worse, due to their engagement in outside projects, none of the Council Committee members except the President even have a regular attendance in the plant, and as a result the Committee never meets and does not, strictly speaking, function.

Even the Council's President devotes more time and energy to experimentation and discovery than to the political tasks of the day. However, it is not because of this that, during the middle of a workday, she is summoned to appear immediately before the organization's leaders. It is not because of the organization of the plant's Council, but rather because of the nature of the plant's productive activity, that the President is summoned to appear before an extraordinary session of the Central Committee of the revolutionary organization. Because she is a worker and also President of an enormous productive enterprise, the organization's leaders treat her with a deference she has frequently found annoying; on numerous occasions she found that excessive cordiality kept them from communicating with her straightforwardly, and she was forced to guess what it was that they actually wanted from her. However, on this occasion the urgent nature of the extraordinary session is im-

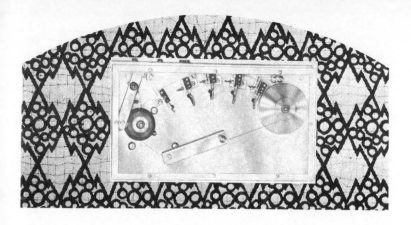

mediately explained to her. The organization's political economist opens the session with a profound analysis of the state of communications technology since the insurrection. Only brief excerpts from his speech can be cited here:

"...—precisely at the historical moment when the revolutionary organization of the working class has successfully seized all the central communications networks—

"—precisely at the historical moment when the primary task of the revolutionary organization is to inform the population of the tasks ahead, to define the needs of the day, to lead and guide the march forward to ever higher forms of working class organization—

"—precisely at the historical moment when the revolutionary organization of the working class most urgently needs the one-way communications media inherited by the working class from the defunct capitalist ruling class—

"—Comrades!—and this is the capital point—it is at this precise historical moment that the masses are abandoning one-way communications media—

"—It is at this precise historical moment that the masses are beginning to use two-way, three-way and many-way electronic devices.

"Comrades—and this is the point of the analysis—these new devices do not only block the air waves and the television channels!

"—What is far more serious is that the new devices distract and mislead the working population; they prevent the clear communication of the slogans and directives regularly broadcast over the central networks.

"The consequences of this chaos-breeding technology are extremely far-reaching. The continuing development of such productive forces becomes a fetter to the revolutionary social relations. This development obstructs the consolidation and concentration of power by the organization of the working class. The working class is no longer informed of the decisions made by the organization of the working class. People are uninformed of the decisions and resolutions

51

passed by the Regional Councils. Even Party members have difficulty keeping up with the organization's political line, with the Party's definition of the tasks of the day. . .

"Comrades, this precise historical moment is a moment of crisis. It is a historical situation which can only be described as a state of total chaos characterized by an alarmingly low level of production, constant shortages—in short, economic stagnation!"

When the political economist finishes his moving speech, the Leader of the organization introduces the President of the electronics plant. "Comrades, in view of this lamentable state of affairs on the eve of the general and universal election of the Central Committee of the Council of All Workers' Councils, we have invited to our session the Comrade President of the electronics enterprise which became justly famous during our glorious revolution for its distribution of walkie-talkies to the struggling workers, an enterprise which was in the vanguard of the revolutionary struggle, which provided a model of revolutionary organization to the entire working class. The Comrade will deepen our understanding of the present lamentable state of affairs, and in particular the Comrade will describe the measures which this important enterprise is taking to combat this state of affairs. Comrade President."

The President sweats and is extremely nervous. She starts to speak in a faltering voice. "The general state of affairs described by our scholarly comrade is indeed lamentable." She is somewhat reassured when numerous Central Committee members nod in agreement. "He has presented an extremely well documented analysis of the general state of affairs." The members nod again. "I am not familiar with the general state of affairs," she continues. "I can only speak of the specific situation in the electronics plant. The scholarly comrade spoke of a low level of production and of constant shortages **in general**. However, at the **specific** level which is familiar to me, namely at the electronics plant, these **general** shortages have not **specifically** manifested themselves. This is not at all a contradiction of the comrade's analysis. I am speaking at an altogether different

52

level of abstraction. My analysis is conditioned by my relation to the productive forces in question. The scholarly comrade's analysis is not subject to such limitations. The further an individual's activity is removed from the productive forces, the less the individual's analysis is conditioned by the development of the productive forces. It is at the level of the superstructure described by the comrade that the state of affairs is indeed lamentable. However, this general condition has not manifested itself at the base. The quantity and variety of the products created in the plant is today several times higher than it was during any of the pre-revolutionary record-breaking periods. Shortages have not manifested themselves either among the inputs or among the outputs. In terms of the outputs: people have either succeeded in designing and producing precisely the products they required, or they found workers in the plant who were willing and ready to design and produce the products. As for inputs: the informal nature of the social relations among productive sectors since the revolution has made possible the establishment of direct contacts among suppliers, producers and users. Nowadays workers themselves contact suppliers of materials, and frequently the workers take part in the production of the specific materials required for a particular project. These direct contacts are often characterized by personality clashes and various forms of acrimony. However, such direct relations do prevent the production and transportation of totally inappropriate materials, which was the rule before the revolution. At the level of abstraction at which I am speaking, namely at the level of the productive activity itself, a low level of production and constant shortages characterized an earlier historical situation—a revolution in which the low production and the shortages were not due to the establishment of direct social relations among the producers, but to the absence of such relations. In this earlier historical situation, shortages resulted from the fact that initiative and decision-making were limited to a small number of planners and party officials who were in general totally divorced from the production process. Comrades, interrupt me if I am wrong. My understanding has always been that the purpose of the Organization is not to stifle the

initiative and self-organization of the working population, but rather to nurse it, to help it grow strong and self-confident, to create the conditions for working people to become the masters of technology and not its slaves."

She pauses. No one nods. There is an icy silence.

"As for the current stage of the struggle," she continues, faltering again, "I can only assure the Comrades that I will do all that is in my power to impress my fellow workers with the importance of the coming elections of the Central Committee. I will see to it that they participate in this critical event."

The Leader of the revolutionary organization deferentially thanks the President of the working collective of the electronics enterprise, "—an enterprise which once marched in the forefront of the working class by supporting and implementing the decisions of the organization of the working class."

The President rushes back to the group with whom she is engaged in a particularly intriguing experiment in communications technology. She is annoyed by the openly exhibited distrust of several individuals who know she has just returned from an important Party meeting. She has frequently in the past been annoyed by individuals who became nervous whenever she began talking about the organizational tasks of the day. On this particular afternoon the relevant slogan—All Power to the Central Committee of the Council of All Workers' Councils—sticks in her throat. She is unable to speak it. The tasks of the current phase of the struggle can no longer be served by her proclamation of the slogan of the day. Perhaps those tasks cannot be realized at the only 'level of abstraction' with which she is familiar, namely at the point of production. Perhaps, she reflects, the realization of those tasks may have to wait until the day when the organization establishes its own State, with an efficient administration, and an army strong enough to enforce the requirements of the day. As for the remainder of this particular afternoon, she abandons herself to the excitement of discovering another new form of multiple-source communications media.

We are forced to conclude that, even under very favorable circumstances, self-organized activity does not provide a fertile field for the growth and success of a revolutionary organization. Independent, self-organized social activity is not, in and of itself, a sufficient condition for the successful seizure of State power by a revolutionary organization. In fact, independent activity seems to hamper the development of such an organization. Consequently, at this point it becomes hard to imagine just what such an organization would have to do in order to seize State power out of such a situation. We can nevertheless try to visualize the organization's attempt to do this.

For example, we might try to imagine the occasion on which the delegates of the working population are to elect the Central Committee of the Council of All Workers' Councils. Such an event might be staged at the National Theater. This setting might be particularly appropriate for numerous reasons. For example, already during the days of the street fighting and the barricades, the National Theater might have been transformed into a continuing public forum. The semi-circular arrangement of the seats, and rows of benches placed on the stage itself, made this auditorium an ideal place for any and all individuals to address themselves to the entire audience. The doors of the theater were open, and the auditorium was crowded, at all hours of the day and night. All schools of philosophical, political, ecological and religious thought could be heard defended by proponents or downgraded by critics. Some individuals read prepared lectures; others spoke off the cuff.

On this occasion, as usual, the auditorium is crowded. An even larger crowd gathers outside the theater. The reason for this extremely large gathering is that organization members, as well as numerous people who have come for the election, add their numbers to the large evening audience which regularly takes part in the open forum. Most organization members are of course impressed by the size of the gathering, especially those who are visiting the forum for the first time, since they assume that all these people have come to observe the scheduled event, the election of the Central Committee. The fact is that most of these people do not know there is a

scheduled event. Their ignorance of the event is not due to lack of preparation or inadequate publicity on the part of the revolutionary organization. On the contrary, the coming election was broadcast hourly over the central radio and television networks and the articles in the organization's newspaper spoke of nothing else. However, the majority of the population has become attracted to new communications devices, and as a result very few people have actually heard the hourly announcements. As for newspapers—they remain on the stands despite the fact that they are now free. No one seems to read them any more; people seem more interested in artistic or technical subjects, and descriptions of unfamiliar or new branches of social activity seem to have replaced the popular magazines and mass circulation newspapers of former days. Even the organization's members did not learn of the event from the mass media of communications; they were personally informed by other members.

The presence of this unexpectedly large crowd creates certain strategic problems for the organizers of the event. Since the public forum is a continuing 24-hour event, the auditorium is already full when the voters arrive. In view of the size of the crowd it would not be practical to ask everyone to leave. The leaders of the organization devise a strategy which, under the circumstances, appears to be the best available alternative. All of the organization's regular People's Marshals are given armbands with the word "Guardian" clearly printed on them, and other hefty members who are not regular Marshals are also given armbands. Some of the Guardians individually approach the people who are sitting on the benches on stage; the marshals explain that a special event is scheduled, and would these people please try to find seats in the auditorium. No one objects; some people find new seats, others leave the theater. The vacated places are then occupied by the arm-banded Marshals. Although the Guardians find themselves continually looked-at by individuals in the auditorium, no one raises a fuss. Other Guardians place themselves at the entrances to the theater, two per door. They allow only individuals with membership cards to enter the theater, explaining to others that the theater is overcrowded and that only people's delegates who are taking part in the special event are being permitted

to enter. Before long, all those who came to attend the important session of the Council of All Workers' Councils are seated in the auditorium.

The next problem is what to do about the large gathering outside the theater. The idea of dispersing this crowd does not appeal to the organization's leaders because a concerted attempt to do this might lead to a riot. This in turn would create bad publicity for the organization. In addition, there is no need to disperse this crowd; it would be much better to give them the opportunity to listen to the deliberations of the Council. Consequently, loudspeakers are placed on the outside walls of the theater.

The stage is now set. The leaders of the revolutionary organization file on to the stage, while the Marshals who had reserved their seats march off. The audience ceases to pay attention to an individual reading a lecture on the fertility of soils in glacial valleys, and all eyes turn to the stage.

The leader of the revolutionary organization walks with dignity to the center of the stage. *"Comrades, we are assembled here as the first conference of the proletarian party, in conditions of revolution and a developing world revolution as well."*

The delegates from the Workers' Councils and Council Committees stand. They are scattered in all parts of the auditorium. They applaud. Others remain seated, and do not applaud.

"I shall begin by referring to a speech which impressed me most. I heard a coal miner deliver a remarkable speech. Without using a single bookish word, he told us how they had made the revolution. Those miners were not concerned with the question as to whether or not they should have a president. They seized the mine, and the important question to them was how to keep the cables intact so that production might not be interrupted. Then came the question of bread, which was scarce, and the miners also agreed on the method of obtaining it. Now that is a real program of the revolution, not derived from books. That is what I call really winning power LOCALLY. We are all agreed that power must be wielded by the Councils of Workers' Deputies. But what can and should they do if power passes to them, i.e., if power is in the hands of the pro-

letarians and semi-proletarians? This is an involved and difficult question. Speaking of the transfer of power, there is a danger--one that played a big part in previous revolutions too--namely, the danger that the revolutionary class will not know what to do with state power when it has won it. The history of revolutions gives us examples of revolutions that failed for this very reason. . . ."

An individual in the auditorium cuts the leader short. "If those revolutions failed, it is because the workers' responses were still conditioned by the social relations. People like you convinced them that what they wanted was State power. And then of course they didn't know what to do with it, because there's nothing at all they can do with it. That's reserved for people like you. Workers who control production don't need State power."

"I can understand the uneducated mass of workers and soldiers naively and unconsciously believing in control," the leader explains. "You only have to think about the fundamental aspects of control, however, to realize that such a belief is a departure from the basic principles of the class struggle. What is control? To control, you must have power." (Numerous organization members applaud. The leader continues.) "The Conference resolves that in order to ensure all the state power passing into the hands of the Councils of Workers' Deputies or other bodies directly expressing the will of the people, prolonged work is necessary to develop proletarian class-consciousness and to unite the urban and rural proletarians against the vacillations of the petit-bourgeoisie, for only work of this nature can guarantee real advance on the part of the whole revolutionary people. This calls for many-sided activity within the Councils of Workers' Deputies, for work aimed at increasing the number of these Councils, consolidating their power, and welding together our Party's proletarian internationalist groups in the Councils."

"Those Party groups aren't as efficient as you make them out to be," shouts someone in the gallery. "Their lack of empathy with other people leads to a profound inability to understand our revolutionary democracy. This inability leads them to dream up policies and measures which are completely out of touch with the social situation."

58

"This is the sum and substance of our policy," says the leader. "The whole petit-bourgeoisie is now wavering and trying to conceal this wavering behind the empty phrase about revolutionary democracy."

The individual in the gallery interrupts again. "Next thing you'll be telling us is that you volunteer to be our new ruler. You ideological officials are subject to acute mental disorders!"

"They all agree," the leader says, "that the Organization will either never dare take over full state power alone, or, if they do dare, and do take power, they will not be able to retain it even for the shortest while. If anybody asserts that the question of the Organization alone taking over full state power is a totally unfeasible political question, that only a swelled-headed 'fanatic' of the worst kind can regard it as feasible, we refute this assertion—"

"Buddy, to do that you'll need an army," shouts the disrupter in the gallery, "and your army'll need an arms industry—and no one I know is about to give you what you need!"

The leader is not disturbed or even annoyed by the continued interruptions, although numerous people in the auditorium are visibly annoyed. "We are concerned now not with the 'day' or 'moment' of insurrection in the narrow sense of the word. That will be only decided by the common voice of those who are in contact with the workers, with the masses. The point is that now, at the Democratic Conference, our party has virtually its own congress, and this congress (whether it wishes to or not) must decide the fate of the revolution."

"So we're to return to that familiar history of princes and kings, pretenders and impostors," shouts the disrupter.

"Having appealed for decisions and not talk, for action and not resolution-writing, we must dispatch our entire group to the factories and the barracks. Their place is there, the pulse of life is there, there is the source of salvation for our revolution. There is no middle course. Delay is impossible. The revolution is dying. By putting the question in this way, by concentrating our entire group in the factories and barracks, we shall be able to determine the right moment to start the insurrection."

"By enriching the power of the State with the power in the factories, you'll be able to determine the right moment to start anything," shouts the heckler in the gallery. And this time numerous other individuals stand up and shout, "Are you serious?" "What is this?"

"Of course," explains the leader, *"this is all by way of example, only to illustrate the fact that at the present moment it is impossible to remain loyal to Marxism, to remain loyal to the revolution unless insurrection is treated as an art."*

"Dictator!" shouts the heckler. "The times when The Leader can lay hold of people's lives are gone!"

"The plea that the proletariat will not be able technically to lay hold of the state apparatus is, perhaps, the most common and most frequent," explains the leader. *"The state apparatus is primarily the standing army, the police and the bureaucracy. By saying that the proletariat will not be able technically to lay hold of this apparatus, the critics reveal their utter ignorance and their reluctance to take into account either facts or the arguments long ago cited in Bolshevik literature."*

The leader suddenly stops and looks up toward the gallery. Soon the eyes of the entire audience are turned toward the gallery. Four sturdy People's Marshals with 'Guardian' armbands have entered the gallery and move toward the heckler. Two Guardians seize the heckler's arms, two seize his legs; they raise the heckler out of his seat and carry him past stunned onlookers. While the Guardians begin to carry the heckler out of the auditorium, the leader continues speaking.

"In addition to the chiefly 'oppressive' apparatus--the standing army, the police and the bureaucracy--the modern state possesses an apparatus which has extremely close connections with the banks and unions, an apparatus which performs an enormous amount of accounting and registration work, if it may be expressed this way. This apparatus must not, and should not, be smashed. It must be expanded, made more comprehensive, and nation-wide. And this can be done by utilizing the achievements already made by large-scale capitalism, in the same way as the proletarian revolution can, in general, reach its goal only by utilizing these achievements."

While speaking, the leader is constantly interrupted by shouts from the heckler as he is carried out of the auditorium. "Fanatic! You're fifty years too late! We haven't gained our own powers in order to give them up to you!" The shouting stops when the Guardians exit from the auditorium, close the door, and apparently carry the heckler outside the theater. There is widespread uneasiness in the audience; numerous individuals turn their heads in all directions, as if looking for an explanation. However, the leader remains perfectly calm, and continues his opening speech as if the incident that just took place had been an expected and pre-planned part of the evening's proceedings.

"The big banks are the 'state apparatus' which we need to bring about socialism, and which we take ready made from capitalism; our task here is merely to lop off what capitalistically mutilates this excellent apparatus, to make it EVEN BIGGER, even more democratic, even more comprehensive. Quantity will be transformed into quality. A single State Bank, the biggest of the big, with branches in every rural district, in every factory, will constitute as much as nine-tenths of the socialist apparatus. This will be country-wide book-keeping, country-wide accounting of the production and distribution of goods, this will be, so to speak, something in the nature of the skeleton of socialist society."

The leader is interrupted again, this time from the ground floor. A large individual with unruly hair and a beard raises his hands high above his head. In a deep voice and pronouncing each word with deliberate care, he appears to be pleading with the audience. "Comrades, do you know what you have done? You, who have rid yourselves of the police, have allowed four self-appointed Guardians to remove a crank, a nuisance, a disrupter. Comrades, you have restored the power of the police. But have you considered who this police will relieve you from next? Perhaps another crank, another disrupter. Perhaps an anarchist. It so happens that I have been an anarchist since—"

While he is speaking, the four Guardians who have surrounded him seize his arms and legs—

As soon as the anarchist is silent, the leader continues his opening speech. *"The Councils will introduce work-books for the whole population."*

"Mark my words!" shouts the anarchist as he is raised out of his seat.

"Every week, or other definite fixed period," continues the leader, *"they will have to get from the union a certificate to the effect that they are performing their work conscientiously; without this they will not be able to receive bread ration cards or provisions in general."*

"The entire old order will be restored in the name of socialism!" shouts the anarchist as he is carried toward the exit.

The leader continues, *"The proletarian state will say: we need good organizers of banking and the amalgamation of enterprises--in this matter the capitalists have more experience, and it is easier to work with experienced people--and we need far, far more engineers, agronomists, technicians and scientifically trained specialists of every kind than were needed before. We shall give all these specialists work to which they are accustomed and which they can cope with; in all probability we shall introduce complete wage equality only gradually and shall pay these specialists higher salaries during the transition period. We shall place them under comprehensive workers' control and we shall achieve the complete and absolute operation of the rule 'He who does not work, neither shall he eat.' We shall not invent the organizational form of the work, but take it ready-made from capitalism--we shall take over the banks, unions, the best factories, experimental stations, academies and so forth; all that we shall have to do is to borrow the best models—"*

At this point at least half the audience have risen from their seats. Another individual on the ground floor begins to speak. "Fellow workers! I am not drunk. I am not a heckler. I am not an anarchist. I am a member of the Revolutionary Organization. I have been a member since long before the revolution. I am here as a Committee delegate to take part in the deliberations of the Council of All Workers' Councils, and in the election of the Central Committee. But I cannot be a party to the proceedings that have just occurred. Such behavior is unprecedented in the practice of our

organization. Today we all know where such procedures will lead. The anarchist comrade's warning is not to be dismissed. This terrorism is initially unleashed on reactionaries. Then it is unleashed on disrupters. All anarchists are disrupters. And who comes next? After the anarchists are removed—"

Numerous Guardians have started to move toward the member of the organization. However, the arm-banded Marshals are unable to reach their destination. Each Guardian is surrounded by a large group of people, who seize the Guardian's arms, then his legs. The individual who was speaking begins to smile, then laugh. "All Power to the People!" she shouts. "All Power to the People" resounds throughout the crowded auditorium. Hundreds of people move toward the exits.

The leader, still calm, appears not to notice that his entire audience is leaving. He concludes the opening speech: *"The line we have marked out is correct, and in the future we shall make every effort to achieve an organization in which there will be no Committee-men to disobey the Central Committee. We are growing, and that is as it should be with a real party."*

The auditorium is absolutely empty. At this point the organization's Central Committee members rise from their seats and begin to file off stage. While they exit, all the Guardians enter at the ground floor and place themselves in military formation in front of the leader, who terminates his opening speech:

*"I declare the All-*Council *Conference open. Please nominate your candidates for election to the Presiding Committee."*

As the leader speaks, a deafening 'All Power to the People' is heard from the outside. This is apparently the crowd's response to the last group of people who exited from the theater. The Guardians had forgotten to turn off the loudspeakers when the proceedings became irregular, and as a result the entire sequence had been broadcast to an immense crowd that had gathered outside the theater.

In response to the leader's opening speech of the Conference, the Guardians click their heels, raise their fists above their heads as if with one motion, and shout perfectly in unison: "All Power to the Leader!"

We have tried to visualize the revolutionary situation as described in the classical revolutionary literature, a situation where *the majority of the working population engage in independent creative work as makers of history,* a situation where *the old centralized government gives way to the self government of the producers.* We have seen numerous confirmations of the classical insight that, in such a situation, *the working people know that in order to work out their own emancipation they have no ideals to realize, but to set free the elements of the new society with which the old collapsing bourgeois society itself is pregnant.* We have seen that *the precondition of any real people's revolution is the break-up, the shattering of the ready-made state machinery.*

However, we have not seen that when *the whole superincumbent strata of official society are sprung into the air* the ground is prepared for the seizure of State power by any type of revolutionary organization. On the contrary, the siutation we have examined suggests precisely the opposite conclusion, namely that *once the majority of the population itself suppresses its oppressors, a 'special force' for suppression is no longer necessary.* Instead of creating the possibility for the seizure of State power, the revolutionary situation destroys this possibility. In fact, the revolutionary situation exposes *the absurdity of combining the words 'freedom' and 'state.' So long as the state exists there is no freedom. When there is freedom there is no state.* Furthermore, the classical revolutionary situation does not even lay the ground for transitional or new forms of State power since, if *labor is emancipated and productive labor ceases to be a class attribute,* and consequently *if the proletariat and the revolutionary democrats do not in fact need a new state apparatus, then the Workers' Councils lose their raison d'etre, lose their right to existence.* In short, *as soon as it becomes possible to speak of freedom the state as such ceases to exist* and it becomes impossible to speak of the seizure of State power.

The revolutionary situation as described by the classical revolutionary theory does not create the necessary conditions for the seizure of State power by revolutionary leaders; on the contrary, we have seen that such a situation destroys the necessary conditions. This conclusion is drastic, but it should not cause undue alarm in the ranks of revolutionary leaders. The conclusion does not say that the project of revolutionary leaders is unrealizable, it merely says that the conditions described by classical revolutionary theory are not in fact the conditions for the realization of this project. It cannot in fact be stated that the project of revolutionary organizations is not historically realizable since such an assertion would fly in the face of hard historical evidence. The seizure of State power by revolutionary leaders is a proved historical possibility. The event which was classically considered to be the necessary condition for this seizure of power is also a historical possibility. All that has been shown so far is that the two events are not related to each other in the way described by classical revolutionary theory.

Our conclusion suggests that classical revolutionary theory saddles revolutionary organizers with a *non sequitur,* that it misinforms them about the nature of the causal relation between two events. It is extremely important for revolutionary leaders to rid themselves of this erroneous assumption about the relation between two key events, since otherwise they will misconceive the very nature of their project and as a result will almost certainly fail. To understand the magnitude of the misconception, we must try to clarify the nature of the classical assumption and to pinpoint the precise nature of the error.

Classical revolutionary theory maintains that the historical possibility of a *revolutionary upsurge,* the historical possibility of universal engagement in *independent creative activity,* is produced by *the development of modern industry* which *cuts from under its feet the very foundation on which the bourgeoisie produces and appropriates products,* and that *therefore what the bourgeoisie produces is its own gravediggers.* Classical revolutionary theory simultaneously maintains that it is historically possible for the leaders of a revolutionary organization to *take state power into their own hands—and if they succeed in taking power, no power on earth can prevent them from retaining it.* The historical possibility of the revolutionary upsurge as well as the historical possibility of the seizure of power are confirmed by social practice. However, classical revolutionary theory does not only maintain that these two events are historically possible, but that they are connected—and not merely connected in the sense that any two events in human society are connected—but that they are causally connected, that one is the necessary condition for the other, that they are two parts of one relation. It is this last proposition that is erroneous. Historical evidence confirms the possibility of revolutionary upsurges of independent creative activity; historical evidence confirms the possibility of seizures of State power; but historical evidence does not confirm the assumed causal connection between the upsurges and the seizures. In fact, the only historically confirmed connection between independent creative activity and the seizure of State power is that references to independent activity, references to the self-government of the producers, frequently appear on the banners of revolutionary organizations that seize State power. But the slogans on the banners are not the precondition for the seizure of power. In fact, we have seen that a real situation which corresponds to the situation described by the slogans does not lay the basis for the seizure of State power but destroys it. The slogans on the banners of revolutionary organizations reflect a misconception, an erroneous assumption, a serious mistake.

We have determined that the classical definition of the conditions for the seizure of State power is erroneous. Our next task is to determine the real conditions for the success of a revolutionary organization. Since the successful seizure of State power by revolutionary organizations is a historical fact, historical conditions for such an event obviously exist. We have not yet determined what those conditions are; so far we have only determined that they are not the classically assumed conditions. However, despite the fact that the real conditions were not explicitly treated by classical revolutionary theory, we can assume that they are implicit in that theory. We can even assume that revolutionary leaders who successfully took State power into their own hands profoundly understood the necessary conditions for their success, even if they did not enrich the classical revolutionary theory with their insights. We can assume that the real conditions for the seizure of power are in fact much more widespread and common than the conditions erroneously defined by the classical theory, if for no other reason than because the seizure of State power by revolutionary organizations has until today been a relatively frequent event, whereas situations of independent creative activity have been extremely rare. In fact, revolutionary organizations have so far succeeded in taking State power over a substantial proportion of the world's population, and no power on earth has prevented them from retaining it. The seizure of State power has become a synonym of 'revolution.' On the other hand, the supposed condition for the seizure of power, independent creative activity by a whole population, has been such a rarity that most of the world's population regards such a situation, not as a historical possibility, but as a slogan on the banners of successful revolutionary organizations — banners which proclaim independence, creativity, and the reappropriation of the self-powers of all by all.

Consequently, if the bourgeoisie cuts its foundation from under its feet by producing its own gravediggers, the bourgeoisie also produces the necessary conditions for the seizure of State power by revolutionary leaders, it also produces the seed of the historically realized forms of Dictatorship of the Proletariat. Our next task is to locate these seeds, to determine the precise nature of the necessary conditions for the seizure of State power.

The real conditions for the seizure of power by revolutionary organizations have been covered up by a mirage. The mirage is composed of images created by classical revolutionary theory—images of *a mighty burst of creative enthusiasm that stems from the people themselves;* images of *the people as the moving force, the creator of universal history, the real heroes;* images of the *unlimited creative power* of *working people engaged in independent creative work as makers of history;* images of *the initiative of millions creating democracy on their own, in their own way — with no ideals to realize but to set free the elements of the new society;* images of *the self-government of the producers,* of *an association in which the free development of each is the condition for the free development of all.*

When we try to approach the mirage, it moves further away, and while moving towards it we continue traversing endless stretches of desert sand. Yet the real conditions for the rise of revolutionary organizations do not reside in the mirage, but precisely in the desert sands from which the mirage diverts our attention. The fact is that *working people engaged in independent creative activity as makers of history* do not create the field for the rise of revolutionary organizations. The fact is that when working people even begin to engage in independent creative activity as makers of history, it is the seizure of State power that becomes a mirage. The fact is that the conditions for the seizure of State power reside in the sands of capitalist daily life, the sands which constitute the normal fabric of bourgeois society, and not in the *mighty burst* which transforms desert sands to soil and trees. The fact is that the seizure of State power **precedes** the mighty burst of independent creative activity because once such activity begins the conditions for the success of revolutionary organizations **no longer** exist.

Independent creative activity may indeed carry the seed of revolutionary organization, just as capitalism carries the seed of its overthrow—but that seed is not itself independence. Independent creative activity on the part of the working population cannot make its historical appearance *without the whole superincumbent strata of official society being sprung into the air.* It is this fact that creates the illusion that it is the independent activity that lays the ground for the seizure of State power. Yet even a superficial glance at the real situation would expose this illusion. If the revolutionary situation is *realized by the initiative of millions creating democracy on their own, in their own way,* if the revolutionary situation is the historical moment when the working population become makers of universal history, then where in the world is the variegated society where millions of imaginations daily create what is original, unexpected and new; where in the world are the populations who create the conditions of life on their own and in their own way? Did they renounce their independence the moment revolutionary organizations seized State power? But in this case it would not be the independence, but rather its renunciation, that paved the way to the seizure of State power. Or did the seizure of State power in fact take place before the entire working population began engaging in independent creative activity as makers of history? But in this case it could not be the independent creative activity that paved the way to the seizure of State power—since it had not yet begun.

If the conditions for the seizure of power exist only during the brief moment after the old order has been *sprung into the air* but before the working population *sets free the elements of the new society,* then serious revolutionary leaders had better be wary of the slogans on their banners. A re-examination of passages in which the classical revolutionary theory explicitly refers to the direct conditions for the seizure of power in fact reveals that all such passages refer to the moment **before** the population begins to engage in independent creative activity. Furthermore, such passages insist that the conditions for the restoration of the old order and the conditions for the seizure of State power exist **only** during this brief moment; they suggest that the next moment, the moment when independent activity becomes generalized to the whole population, will be too late for the seizure of State power: *The Bolsheviks must take power at once--otherwise a wave of real anarchy may become stronger than we are.* The seizure must take place *before a mighty burst of creative enthusiasm stems from the people themselves,* before the population gains confidence in its *unlimited creative powers,* before the moment when *a wave of real anarchy* sweeps away the conditions necessary for the restoration of the old order, the conditions necessary for the seizure of State power.

The moment which contains the conditions for the seizure of State power, the moment on which revolutionary leaders must rely and during which they must act if they are to succeed, is not the moment when the population gains confidence in its own self-powers, in its creative capacities. On the contrary, *the insurrection must rely upon that turning point in the history of the growing revolution -- when the vacillations in the ranks of the weak, half-hearted and irresolute friends of the revolution are strongest.* This is not a moment of self-confidence; it is the moment when *the people are close to desperation,* the moment when *that most painful thing on earth, vacillation, has worn the people out.*

The moment for the seizure of power is not a moment of independence, but of anxiety in the face of independence. It is the moment when people are on the verge of independence, when they reach the frontier between the known and the unknown, between the familiar and the new--and temporarily recoil. It is the moment when all the official authorities have been sprung into the air, but when society's individuals have not yet actively appropriated the powers they had vested in the deposed authorities. It is the moment when only one part of the dominant social relation has been sprung into the air—the superincumbent strata; but when the other part of the same social relation—the subordination, the dependence, the helplessness—has not yet been sprung. It is the moment when the frontier between dependence and independence—precisely because it has not yet been crossed—appears to be an unbridgeable chasm. And it is precisely at this frontier, alongside the human beings who are about to cross it, alongside the *true agents of the revolution,* that the revolutionary frontier officials, the leaders, take their positions. *In every revolution there intrude, alongside its true agents, men of a different stamp; some of them survivors of and devotees to past revolutions, without insight into the present movement, but preserving popular influence by their known honesty and courage, or by sheer force of tradition; others mere brawlers, who, by dint of repeating year after year the same set of stereotyped declarations against the government of the day, have sneaked into the reputation of revolutionists of the first water. As far as their power goes, they hamper the real action of the working class, exactly as men of that sort have hampered the full development of every previous revolution.* But while hampering the real action of the working class, they pave their own way to the seizure of State power. The successful seizure of power by revolutionary leaders is assured only during the moment before the working class appropriates its powers; it is possible only because the population has **not yet** become independent: *Our victory is assured because the people are close to desperation.* It is only during the moment before confidence sets in that the leaders of a revolutionary organization *have the exceptional advantage of a situation in which only our victory in the insurrection can put an end to that most painful thing on earth, vacillation, which has worn the people out.*

If revolutionary leaders are to seize the moment when a breach in the social order creates the conditions for their success, they must recognize the error of classical revolutionary theory, they must free themselves of the illusion that their rise coincides with the rise of independent creative activity. If they cling to this illusion and postpone their decisive blow until the moment when independent activity begins, they may well pass up their last chance to take State power into their own hands. The moment which contains the conditions for their success is very brief, whereas the following moment *a wave of real anarchy may become stronger than* they are—and this *wave of real anarchy* may well be the beginning of a process as irreversible as the transition from hunting to agriculture. If a dependent population crossed the frontier to independence, it would remove the conditions for the restoration of the old order, it would no longer need subordination, control or managers, it would destroy the conditions for the seizure of State power by revolutionary leaders.

The preliminary conditions for the seizure of State power are not in fact conditions for the overthrow of the dominant social order, as classical revolutionary theory would have us believe, but conditions for the restoration of the dominant social order. The moment before independent creative activity begins contains the necessary conditions for both the seizure of State power and the restoration of the old order, and these conditions are in fact the same. These conditions are created by a situation in which the authorities, managers, officials and guards are already gone, but the desperation, vacillation, anxiety and fear are still there. These conditions exist only during the brief moment after the objective relations of dependence are removed, but before the subjective consequences of these relations are removed. These facts have been admitted by successful revolutionary leaders—if they had not known them they could not have succeeded. *Insurrection must rely upon the vacillations in the ranks of the weak, half-hearted and irresolute.* But this insight has not replaced *the mighty burst of creative enthusiasm, the unlimited creative powers of the real heroes,* which are carried on the banners of revolutionary organizations to this day. If the project of revolutionary organizations is to remain viable, revolutionary leaders must erase the illusions of the classics from the banners and replace them with a slogan that describes the real conditions for the successful seizure of State power: *We want the socialist revolution with people as they are now, with people who cannot dispense with subordination, control and managers.*

People who cannot dispense with managers **after** the managers have been sprung into the air are people who carry their managers within themselves, people who have internalized the officials. People who cannot dispense with control **after** the physical and intellectual police forces have been sprung into the air are people who have dried up their imaginations, stunted their own self-powers, people who, lacking the possibility, lost the ability to decide and move on their own. People who cannot dispense with subordination *after the whole superincumbent strata of official society have been sprung into the air* are human beings who do not consider themselves full human beings, who see themselves through the eyes of their 'superiors' as inferior, as subordinates, as slaves. For *people as they are now,* the **absence** of subordination, control and managers creates fear, anxiety, despair and desperation, *it creates that most painful thing on earth, vacillation*—and these are precisely the real conditions for the successful seizure of State power, for it is precisely when *the people are close to desperation* that *Our victory is assured.*

The preliminary condition for the rise of revolutionary leaders is not the independence which dispenses with the need for subordination, control and managers, but the dependence which cannot dispense with them.

The precondition for the seizure of State power is the mass psychology of dependence. The need for revolutionary organizations and leadership arises, not from self-confidence created by independent activity, but from adaptation to dependence. This need arises when an individual internalizes the superincumbent strata of official society, when an individual adapts to socially created conditions of material scarcity, when an individual submits to social relations of subordination. And the need for leadership is the greater the more the individual derives positive enjoyment from the internalizations, the adaptations, the submission. The conditions for the success of revolutionary organizations exist only during the brief moment after the population has expropriated the ruling classes, but when the population has not yet actively appropriated the productive forces—when the active appropriation of the productive forces has not yet conquered the mass psychology of dependence, the anxiety, the fear, the *desperation* which is the sign for the leader's battlecry: *Our victory is assured!*

The mass psychology of dependence—*people who cannot dispense with subordination, control and managers*—this is the real condition for the seizure of power by a revolutionary organization. Although this condition results from the various ways people adapt to the dominant social order, in normal times it cannot easily be distinguished from the routines of daily life. The mass psychology of dependence becomes visible when an extraordinary event suspends or disrupts its normal reproduction, because at such moments it gives rise to fear, anxiety and desperation.

70

When the guards suddenly disappear, but when people have not yet exercised their freedom, what strikes fear into their hearts? What drives them to the point of desperation? What causes *that most painful thing on earth, vacillation, which wears the people out?*

During the course of normal times, one had to rise at a given hour, to be at a given place at a given time, in order to survive. And even then survival was not assured. Even people who did as they were told were constantly being removed, excluded, deprived. One lost all desires except one: not to be deprived. One lost all projects except one: to rise at the given hour so as to be at the given place, at the given time. This project had become one's entire habit structure, one's personality. And one day when one is there, at the given place, at the given hour—and the guard doesn't come, and continues not to come—is it the end? Fear grips one's heart; the daily anxiety one had learned to accept as a normal part of life gives way to desperation; one cannot dispense with the subordination, the control—

If one could not suppress all of one's desires, if one wanted more than the common lot, where could one get more if not from the others? One had to learn the fears of this one, the weaknesses of another; one had to learn ways to protect the weak, ways to alleviate fears—and to charge for one's services. One even had to create obstacles and hardships so as to be paid for alleviating them. One was called a cheat, a thief, an impostor—but what did it matter? One's lot was incomparably better, one's meals incomparably richer. One who was a cheat or a thief was better off; the designations became titles. Can all this suddenly end? Wouldn't this sudden collapse put one's whole being in question? If one can no longer have more, how can one be more than the common lot? No, one wants people as they are now—

One had no self. One had a given place in the line, and that was all. Yet how one longed to be someone, how one longed to be recognized as someone, as more than a place in a line! And how could one earn this recognition, how could one become someone, except by submitting to tasks no one else submitted to? One was called a traitor, a scab—by whom? By self-less nobodies, by those who were nothing more than places in the line. One became indifferent to their tags, their insults. What mattered was how one was seen by those outside, how one was rewarded by the Authorities. What mattered was that one had become someone; one had gained recognition and self-esteem. What mattered was that one had become an extension of the Authorities, one had become superior to the others, the inferiors; one was no longer a self-less shadow; one's self glowed in the light reflected by the Authorities; one learned to appreciate one's self through the eyes of the Authorities. All this was absolutely necessary: how could one have survived without recognition, without some affirmation of one's importance? One couldn't; one's adaptation was, after all, only human. And after one has effaced oneself so successfully, after one has internalized the Authorities so thoroughly that nothing else remains inside one, how can one believe even for an instant that the authorities have disappeared? One cannot stomach such a possibility. Could it mean that one has ceased to be what one is, that one has disappeared? Are the others suddenly one's equals—and has one, after all, been nothing more than a scab? It is not vacillation that wears one out. It is hysteria. No, one cannot dispense with subordination—

Of course one was always free to make one's own decisions, any decisions, at any time of day or night. One merely had to think them. One could decide to look into the sun or away from it, to shut one's eyes or to open them. Every decision was permitted, so long as one rose at the given hour, so long as one was at the given place at the given time. The field for decision-making was boundless. Why should one also have wanted to decide what one had no power to decide? How could one have learned to make decisions that one never made? When to rise, where to go, what to do, how, why, with whom—these matters were never within one's reach, one never had the ability to make such decisions. Yet one day the official decision-makers are sprung into the air. When is one to rise, where should one go, what should one do, how, why, with whom? No, one cannot dispense with managers.

One lugged stones uphill, under orders. One lugged them back down, under orders. One engaged with others in any number of

projects, under orders. The projects were not created, invented; they were the normal daily routine; they were the official projects which were performed before one arrived and continued to be performed after one left. When one was not under orders, one did not engage in projects with others, one could not even conceive of projects which were not carried out under orders. Could one have imagined unofficial projects as anything other than an extension of the daily routine into one's free hours? Could they have meant anything more than a useless waste of time and energy? When one was not engaged in official activity one did nothing. And is it the official project, the daily routine, the working day, the job, that suddenly explodes? Does one suddenly have to initiate a project with others so as not to miss a meal? Does one suddenly have to invent the content of every single minute of the living day? How is one to begin, and with whom? What is one to experience if not fear, desperation? No, one cannot dispense with managers.

Dehumanization, degradation, self-negation—these were mere words. One was not put ill at ease when these words were spoken. Why should one have been disturbed? Was it one's fault? Had one chosen to be here? Really? Had one seen everything 'outside'—and then chosen to come in here, so as to degrade and dehumanize oneself? What did such words mean? After all, one did not choose to come here. One was born here. And one became whatever it was possible for one to become here. One who had never been 'outside', who had never been 'humanized', could not have become 'de-humanized.' How could one compare oneself to what one could have been 'outside' when one could not even imagine an 'outside'? One's imagination remained 'inside'—it couldn't be stretched any further. One was what one was, and that was all one could imagine oneself to be. And if everything one was is suddenly sprung into the air, is one really expected to run—where? Outside? What kind of 'outside'? An 'outside' no one believes is there, an 'outside' that one cannot even imagine? Why should one run? What can one expect 'outside' other than subordination, control, managers, and men as they are 'inside'?

Nothing was really unbearable, really unsupportable. Everything

was arranged quite efficiently, everything functioned fairly well, everything was planned intelligently enough. One was in fact able to enjoy numerous moments of peace and quiet, to sleep in relative calm without being disturbed. All in all one was able to enjoy a certain comfort. In exchange for the peace, the quiet and the comfort, much was not really demanded of one. Of course one had to abide by the prevailing rules and regulations, one had to obey the laws. But one did not consider this an encroachment, an imposition. After all, everyone else abided by the same rules. This was merely normal, conventional behavior. And for this, one was rewarded with conventional recognition, conventional comforts—and above all with peace and quiet. Yet suddenly, without warning, without explanation, one is robbed of this merely average comfort. Suddenly nothing is arranged, nothing is planned. Suddenly the intelligence that had taken everything in hand explodes. Suddenly there are neither rules nor regulations nor conventional rewards—but one cannot dispense with these if one only wants to find peace and quiet, if one wants to sleep without being disturbed. No, one cannot dispense with them—

And it should be mentioned that one was able to do more than obey the laws passively. One could, if one desired, enforce the laws. In fact the authorities actively encouraged one to do this. And one's prerogatives were nearly unlimited—not in dispensing the rewards, but in dispensing the punishments. This did not make the situation merely bearable; it made it positively enjoyable. One did not only derive joy from one's position, one's prestige, one's power; one derived it most of all from inflicting the punishments. And it should be pointed out that the main punishments were not physical. It was extremely difficult to break an individual's will by physical means. The main instruments were mental; the greatest pain was inflicted by defining, grading, and comparing the victim; by making others see the victim as an object, a thing—until at last the victim broke and became a thing to itself. So what if the whole situation suddenly explodes? Should one fear the revenge of all one's past victims? Only if one has not been successful in breaking their will permanently. Should one fear for oneself? Perhaps, but the moment can hardly be expected to

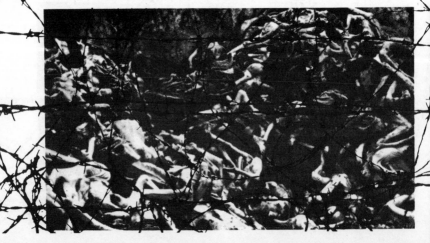

last. The new leaders will certainly not dispense with the various types of law enforcers ready to serve them: how else could they expect people to abide by their rules and regulations? No, the new leaders will not dispense with experienced police officers; they will need more of them; how else will they enforce their revolutionary program?

And lest it be thought that the whole experience consisted of a constant waiting, an endless boredom, it should be pointed out that opportunities for adventure, for risky and romantic undertakings, were not lacking. Furthermore, such undertakings were highly esteemed by the Authorities, and one was sumptuously rewarded. Such undertakings required the talents of a performer, the flexibility of an acrobat and the knowledge of a philosopher. One had to ingratiate oneself with a circle of schemers, pass oneself off as one of them, push their own scheme further and further—until the authorities decided to cut the scheme short by liquidating the schemers. Philistines called the practitioners of this vocation 'informers,' although 'information experts' would have been more appropriate for conveying the talents, the flexibility and the knowledge required for this discipline. In any case, the Philistines were quickly removed. As for this bursting into air, this explosion: it can affect only the top officials; has there ever been a revolution that dispensed with information experts?

Not only one's activities and habits, but also one's morality was based on subordination and control. After all, one was not an animal, one could not simply allow oneself to be harnessed to the cart and whipped to run. One had to justify the submission. One did not obey for the sake of obeying. Obedience was not merely necessary or prudent. Obedience was Good. Furthermore the moral were rewarded, the immoral punished. If an individual who had not disobeyed the laws was nevertheless punished, the punishment itself proved that the individual was bad, morally depraved. If that were not the case, if the Authorities acted arbitrarily and punished individuals according to unpredictable whims, the situation would have been unbearable. One would have lived in constant fear. One

could not dispense with morality. One had to assume that the Authorities punished only the bad—and for one's peace of mind one had to see to it that the Authorities punished anyone who visibly broke a law, no matter how modestly. Only thus could the moral rest assured that they would only be rewarded. The assurance that they, the moral, would not be unjustly punished, demanded that the immoral be justly punished. Those who refused to carry out their conventional assignments had to be the ones who were materially deprived. Those who rebelled against the Authorities had to be the ones who were ostracised, excluded. Those who broke the laws had to be subjected to physical pain and incarceration. Those who tried to rise up against the Authorities had to be starved, killed, removed. How else could the law-abiding be assured that the moral would not be deprived, ostracised, tortured, jailed, or put to death? And if this ever happened—if the moral were tortured, jailed or killed—one had to find a scapegoat, one had to point one's finger at a criminal whose evil presence was what made the Authorities punish the innocent. Official society may well be sprung into the air in one moment. But what of morality? That will not spring into the air until the social practice on which it is based gives way to an altogether different practice. In the meantime, one cannot dispense with the Authorities, the criminals, or the scapegoats.

The ultimate justification for submission and self-negation had been the function of the morality of ulterior aims and higher purposes. Ultimately, one never submitted, one never bowed or crawled, for the sake of the rewards. Ultimately one's self-negation was a noble act of sacrifice and suffering; one degraded oneself for the sake of the family, for the sake of the children—so that they, too, might degrade themselves, suffer and sacrifice themselves for the sake of the Good and the Right. One cannot dispense with suffering and sacrifice, for how else can one be exalted? In the absence of a morality of ulterior aims and higher purposes, where would Law, Order and Civilization derive their justifications? Clearly, one cannot dispense with suffering and sacrifice, with submission and self-negation, with subordination, control and managers. *No, we want the socialist revolution with people as they are now—*

The preliminary condition for the seizure of State power by a revolutionary organization is not independent creative activity; it is fear, anxiety and desperation in the face of independent creative activity; it is the mass psychology of dependence. The moment for the seizure of State power is the moment before independent activity begins. The moment when the old order springs into the air, people do not immediately engage their *unlimited creative powers,* they do not immediately become *the makers of history,* because this requires a complete break with *all the muck of ages,* with all past history. They are gripped by anxiety—an anxiety that could only be conquered by independent creative activity, by social practice. But the anxiety itself keeps them from acquiring the experience that could conquer the anxiety. A modest illustration might clarify this dilemma. Let us imagine the case of an individual who grew up under strict supervision, perhaps because a parent was overly protective, or perhaps as part of a psychologist's experiment. Let us suppose that the supervisor suddenly leaves, or dies. The individual will probably panic—the first moment. Dependence on the supervisor has become part of the individual's very being, and the sudden absence of the supervisor drives the individual to the point of desperation. If the individual began to decide on her, or his, own, the hysteria would gradually subside; if the individual began to move independently, the anxiety would gradually disappear. However, the Doctor takes the individual under his wing when the anxiety is at its highest point, when it is at the point of desperation and hysteria. The Doctor cures the anxiety by providing the individual with the supervision the individual could not dispense with. The revolutionary leader plays the same historical role as the Doctor in this example. The illustration clarifies a point whose importance for revolutionary leaders cannot be exaggerated. If the Doctor had arrived only a brief moment later, the individual would no longer have responded to the cure; the individual would have started to gain confidence in self-powers—desire, ability, imagination—that the individual did not know were available, because he or she had never exercised them. This is why it is so critical for the revolutionary organization to seize power precisely at the right moment. The fact is that the following moment, the moment of independence, the moment when it is already too late to administer the revolutionary cure—this second moment is never very far off. The fact is that the conquest of fear and anxiety through independent practice is a very commonplace event. The fact is that almost every child in contemporary society grows up under relatively strict supervision, and most of these individuals leave their supervisors at one or another point in their lives. If they panic, if the absence of the supervisor drives them to the point of desperation, the fact is that this anxiety only lasts for a moment—the first moment. As soon as they begin to decide on their own, to move independently, the anxiety disappears. Even entire communities are known to have panicked when important supervisors—Chiefs or Priests on whose presence the wellbeing of the community depended—suddenly disappeared, and the fact is that such communities are not known to have missed even one meal because of the absence of the indispensable personage. The moment is very brief.

If through social practice each individual became confident in his or her own self-powers, there would no longer be a field in which revolutionary leaders could grow and succeed. If social activity were allowed to become what each individual independently and creatively makes it, then each of society's individuals would define the aims and purposes of social life and these aims and purposes could not be the program of a revolutionary organization. If social tasks were defined by the desires and imaginations of each, and if they were realized by the self-powers of each, then the Party could not define social tasks nor the State realize them. If society's individuals appropriated their self-powers from the officials who represent these powers, if they snatched their decision-making powers from the personifications who embody and wield these powers in their name, then revolutionary leaders, *i.e., the representatives of revolutionary proletarian inter-nationalism,* could not *embody in their policy the idea that is motivating countless working people all over the world. —All this is elementary. All this is simple and clear. Why replace this by some rigmarole? —If we seize power today, we seize it not in opposition to the Councils but on their behalf.* —If we seize power tomorrow, we might have to seize it on our own behalf, in opposition to the entire working population.

The independent practice that would put an end to the mass psychology of dependence cannot take place once the organization seizes power. The seizure of power by the revolutionary organization puts an end to the anxiety and desperation which gripped the population when dependence relations were disrupted. The seizure and restoration of the State saves people from having to discover and invent the power of community after thousands of years of alienated community, of law and order, of Civilization. Fear in the face of the unfamiliar, anxiety in the face of the unknown, hysteria in the face of the inexperienced, subside in the reassuring warmth of familiar, known, experienced social relations. Aims are restored to the aimless, direction to the directionless, order to the disarrayed. The shepherd returns to sheep gone astray. People who could not dispense with subordination, control and managers are given subordination, control and managers. Conditions of scarcity are re-established for those whose whole being had been shaped in response to such conditions, together with rewards for conformity and punishments for independence. A morality of ulterior aims and higher purposes—the family, the children, and the Nation—justifies the submission required by the struggle for survival. Above all, individuals with Good Politics are assured that the authorities are just, that they punish only individuals with Bad Politics. To give assurance to the Good, scapegoats are provided by the authorities. *Who are our friends and who are our enemies?--this is a question of fundamental importance to the revolution.* The void is eliminated. Anxiety ends. The people are no longer *close to desperation* because *we are showing the entire population a sure way out; we demonstrate to the entire population the value of our leadership. Only our victory can put an end to that most painful thing on earth, vacillation, which has worn the people out.* The people can now relax. The desires and imaginations of the people need no longer be exerted to invent relations, tasks, projects, since their self-powers have no field where they can be exercised. The goal has been realized. *State power has passed into the hands of the organ of the Council of Workers' and Soldiers' Deputies--the Revolutionary Military Committee, which heads the proletariat and the garrison.*

The seizure of State power by the revolutionary organization responds to the needs of *people who cannot dispense with subordination, control and managers.* At the same time, the revolutionary organization itself needs *people as they are now, people who cannot dispense with subordination.* The mass psychology of dependence is the condition to which the seizure of State power responds, and also the condition which it requires.

Why, then, does classical revolutionary theory describe precisely the opposite as the condition for the seizure of State power? If the condition is dependence, why does classical theory point to independence? This seems like a paradox only if it is thought that the classical revolutionary theory is a single, unitary theory of revolution. The paradox disappears as soon as it is understood that the classical theory contains two separate and distinct theories of revolution. One is a theory of the class structure of capitalism and the conditions for its overthrow. The other is a theory of revolutionary organization and the conditions for its seizure of power. The two events are distinct; their necessary conditions are distinct. Paradox and confusion have been created by the historical treatment of one event as if it were the other, and by the treatment of the necessary conditions for one event as if they were necessary conditions for the other. Classical revolutionary theory does in fact contain a very precise description of the necessary conditions for the seizure of State power, a description which pinpoints the mass psychology of dependence as the necessary condition. But this description is couched in the language of the other theory, in the language of independence, and as a result the true import and content of this description have been obscured.

The theory of the class structure of capitalist society is not a theory of revolutionary organization. It is a theory which defines social classes, not in terms of their relation to a revolutionary organization, but in terms of their relation to society's means of production. One class is characterized by its subordination to the other, a subordination which takes the form of alienation of all decision-making powers. The other class is characterized by its control over the first, a control which takes the form of direction and management of all of society's activities. It is only in the frame of reference of this theory that the destruction of the dependence relation itself is the preliminary condition for revolution. *A revolution can be successfully carried out only if the majority of the working population engage in independent creative activity as makers of history.* Independent creative activity by the majority of the working population is the necessary as well as the sufficient condition for the overthrow of the class structure of capitalism because *the proletariat, the lowest stratum of our present society, cannot stir, cannot raise itself up, without the whole superincumbent strata of official society being sprung into the air.*

On the other hand, the theory of revolutionary organization is not a theory of class structure. In the frame of reference of this theory, the destruction of dependence relations is not a condition for the seizure of State power by the revolutionary organization. We have already shown that the seizure of State power cannot be successfully carried out if the majority of the working population engage in independent creative activity as makers of history. We have also shown that the seizure of State power can be successfully carried out only if the majority of the working population do not engage in independent creative activity as makers of history, only if dependence relations—subordination, control and, management—remain intact. We will now show that the classical revolutionary theory contains a very precise description of the conditions for the successful seizure of power by revolutionary organizations, and that the identification of these conditions with independent creative activity is historically unfounded.

The classical theory which defines the real conditions for the revolutionary organization's seizure of power is not the theory of class structure but the **theory of class consciousness.** This is a theory which defines the revolutionary class, not in terms of its relation to society's means of production, but in terms of its relation to the revolutionary organization. According to the theory of class consciousness, individuals or social classes are revolutionary if they adhere to revolutionary ideas, to revolutionary thought, to revolutionary ideology, to the program of the revolutionary organization.

80

The theory of class consciousness and the theory of class structure do not have the same frame of reference. This is obscured by the fact that one theory borrows language from the other, and thus refers linguistically to the same frame of reference. But except for terminological similarities, the two theories have nothing in common. Both theories refer to the working class, the proletariat, as the revolutionary class—but the same terms do not in reality refer to the same subjects in the two theories. Those who are revolutionary according to one theory are not necessarily proletarians according to the other, and those who are proletarians according to the second theory are not necessarily revolutionary according to the first.

According to the theory of class consciousness, individuals can be considered class conscious revolutionaries even if they would not be classified as proletarians by the theory of class structure, namely in terms of their relation to society's means of production. In fact, the most class conscious of revolutionaries, the leaders of the revolutionary organization, *the representatives of revolutionary proletarian internationalism* who *have embodied in their policy the idea that is motivating countless working people all over the world,* would not be defined as proletarians by the theory of class structure. These class conscious revolutionaries have been *educated representatives of the propertied classes, intellectuals; by their social status they belonged to the bourgeois intelligentsia.* Furthermore, *the working class, exclusively by its own effort, is able to develop. . . nothing more nor less than consciousness in an embryonic form.* In other words, according to the theory of class consciousness, those who are conscious revolutionaries are not only themselves not members of the working class, but the working class itself cannot become fully conscious. In fact, in the theory of class consciousness, the relation of individuals to the means of production is completely irrelevant. With the theory of consciousness it is possible to characterize *the proletariat* as *actually becoming more and more bourgeois,* as *prisoners of bourgeois ideology,* and even as having *deserted to the bourgeoisie.* Such characterizations would be meaningless in the theory of class structure, since in the frame of reference of this theory a *proletariat* that *had deserted to the bourgeoisie* could only have done so by appropriating the means of production, an event that cannot take place *without the whole superincumbent strata being sprung into the air.*

According to the theory of consciousness, whether or not an individual or a class is revolutionary depends on the presence or absence of revolutionary consciousness in that individual or class. At first glance this appears to be a form of idealism. However, this appearance is only another result of the confusion between the theory of class structure and the theory of consciousness. It is only in appearance that the theory of consciousness maintains that revolution grows out of ideas in people's heads. This appearance is created by using the word 'revolution' in the place of 'seizure of State power,' and the appearance is magnified into a hallucination by an intentional association of the word 'revolution' with the *independent creative activity* described by the other theory. It is only because of this intentional confusion that a bizarre sequence of *non-sequiturs* parades as a set of axioms ideally suited for slogans, viz. that the thoughts of the organization's leader in people's heads make them revolutionary, therefore also independent and creative, and that as the level of these thoughts rises, the dominant social order falls. These propositions are axioms for people who are willing and able to believe them, and belief in these propositions is in fact a sign that the believer possesses a relatively high level of consciousness. However, the theory of class consciousness has been primarily an instrument for the seizure of State power by revolutionary leaders, and only secondarily a set of articles of faith. It is the primary function of the theory that concerns us here. The primary function of the theory of consciousness has been to define for aspiring leaders the real conditions for the seizure of State power, and in defining these real conditions the theory of class consciousness has been idealistic only in appearance.

As an analysis of the conditions for the seizure of power by revolutionary leaders, the theory of class consciousness is no more idealistic than the theory of class structure. Both theories are equally materialistic. Both theories are equally about social relations. But they are not about the same social relations. The theory of class structure is about the relations between capitalists and laborers, about the conditions for the overthrow of these relations. The theory of class consciousness is about the relations between an organization and a mass, about the conditions for the organization's seizure of power over the mass.

The theory of class consciousness defines people in terms of their thoughts instead of their practice, in terms of their ideology instead of their social relations, only in appearance. It does not define them in terms of the social relations described by the theory of class structure. But it defines them in terms of social relations nevertheless. To define social classes in terms of their ideas would require reading the minds of countless individuals; mind-reading is not in fact the method by which the class-consicous are defined. In reality, the presence or absence of class consciousness is determined by the practice of an individual or a class; it is determined by the presence or absence of specific social relations. The level of an individual's consciousness is measurable, not by the number of correct revolutionary thoughts which show on the individual's forehead, but by the extent to which the individual is a follower of the organization, by the real, concrete activity of attending meetings and demonstrations, carrying out assignments, obeying orders. The more regularly the individual attends organization meetings and events, the more unflinchingly the individual carries out assignments, the more unquestioningly the individual obeys orders, the higher the individual's level of consciousness. The level of consciousness of a social class is measurable, not by the number of revolutionary thoughts protruding from heads, but by the number of individuals of the class who are Party members, by the extent to which the members of a class adhere to the revolutionary organization.

Class consciousness may be an attribute of an individual or a social class. It refers to the presence or absence of ideas. But its presence or absence can only be determined by the social practice of the individual or class, by the presence or absence of concrete social relations. These social relations are specific relations between an individual and a revolutionary organization, and between a class and a revolutionary organization. The individuals who have the highest level of consciousness, the *representatives of proletarian internationalism,* the leaders, are not themselves members of the revolutionary class but are *educated representatives of the propertied classes.* The class itself *is able to develop nothing more than consciousness in an embryonic form.* The class depends on the leaders for its level of consciousness, its revolutionary essence, which in practice means that the revolutionary essence of the working class depends on the extent to which workers submit to the will of leaders.

The social relations behind class consciousness are social relations between leaders and followers, social relations of subordination and control. They are dependence relations. What is meant by class conscious masses is people who submit to the will of a revolutionary leader, people who cannot dispense with subordination, control and managers. Class consciousness is a euphemism for the mass psychology of dependence.

The theory of class consciousness is a theory of social relations which describes the real conditions for the seizure of State power by a revolutionary organization. It describes as necessary conditions precisely those conditions which correspond to the mass psychology of dependence. In spite of its linguistic obscurities, the theory is a very precise instrument for locating the conditions for the seizure of power, for identifying followers of the revolutionary organization, for distinguishing the revolutionary leader's friends from the leader's enemies—which is the *question of fundamental importance to the revolution.*

We have seen that the theory of class consciousness explicitly defines followership, submission, the mass psychology of dependence, and not *independent creative activity,* as the preliminary condition for the growth of the revolutionary organization. Once this is clear, it can also be seen that the theory of class consciousness explicitly excludes independent creative activity as a condition for the rise of revolutionary organization and leadership. It must be remembered that the theory has been of service to countless leaders who successfully seized State power, and that this service could not have been performed by a theory which systematically misguided them. The rejection of *independent creative activity* is so thoroughly couched in the language of the theory of class structure that it is nearly incomprehensible to the layman, but it has nevertheless been clear and explicit to astute revolutionary leaders who seriously aspired to seize power.

The rejection of the *independent creative activity* of the *majority of the working people* in a language which affirms the independent creative activity of the majority of the working people required a complete overhaul of words and concepts, an overhaul which involved nothing less than the transformation of the meanings of words and concepts into their opposites. The theory of class consciousness borrows the entire vocabulary with which the theory of class structure had characterized the bourgeoisie, the proletariat and the revolution—and it applies this entire encyclopedia of words and concepts to the field of leaders and followers, the field of revolutionary organization and revolutionary masses. It is this shift of fields that requires a complete shift of meanings. In the theory of class consciousness, bourgeoisie and proletariat are not described in terms of their relation to means of production; they are defined in terms of their relation to the revolutionary organization.

The theory of class consciousness defines the working class, the proletariat, as the revolutionary class. The words are borrowed from the analysis of class structure, but they are infused with new meanings. The theory proceeds by defining *class conscious workers* as revolutionary. However, since the working class itself, *exclusively by its own effort,* cannot become fully conscious, and therefore cannot become fully revolutionary, there is a stratum which is more conscious and more revolutionary, the vanguard of the working class, the representatives of the revolutionary proletariat. And it is also said that the representatives of the proletariat are not themselves proletarians; they are bourgeois intellectuals. At first glance the purpose of this logic is hard to understand, since it leads to the bizarre conclusion that the only truly revolutionary proletarians are *educated representatives of the propertied classes, intellectuals.* The same transformation of meanings takes place when the working class itself is characterized. First of all there are two types of workers, two types of proletarians. Workers who adhere to the organization, attend meetings and carry out orders, are a class conscious revolutionary mass base, and are therefore by implication independent, creative and courageous. However, workers who act on their own, creatively, independently of the initiative, guidance or direction of the revolutionary organization, are said to act *spontaneously*. This 'spontaneous element' in essence represents nothing more nor less than consciousness in an embryonic form. In other words, their consciousness is not yet born. If such workers remain independent, if they are not taken under the wing of the revolutionary organization, they will be encircled *on every side with a petty-bourgeois atmosphere, which permeates and corrupts the proletariat and causes constant relapses among the proletariat into petty-bourgeois spinelessness, disunity, individualism, and alternate moods of exaltation and dejection.* Such workers may *become more and more bourgeois* until finally they become *prisoners of bourgeois ideology* and *desert to the bourgeoisie.* The working class, as defined by the theory of class structure, has been the majority of the population in highly developed industrial regions. However, since in these regions revolutionary organizations have not seized power, this working population has not been a class conscious revolutionary mass base; it has therefore been *bourgeois, a prisoner of bourgeois ideology,* and a *deserter to the bourgeoisie.* At first glance this logic is as bizarre as the first, and we are left with the paradoxical conclusion that the only truly revolutionary proletarians are bourgeois intellectuals, and that the proletarians themselves are by and large bourgeois.

The logic of the theory of consciousness is meaningless only if it is understood within the framework of the theory of class structure. But the logic does not lack significance. Its significance is military. The theory of consciousness does not describe relations between the social classes of capitalist society, but relations between soldiers and their commanders, relations between armies and general staffs. Although the language refers to dialectical logic, social classes, and socialist revolution, the frame of reference has nothing in common with the subject matter of German philosophy, English political economy or French socialism. It is a much older frame of reference. It is a theory of leaders and followers, friends and enemies. The language borrowed from the theory of class structure serves a moral function: its purpose in the theory of consciousness is to inspire loyalty toward the friends and hatred toward the enemies; the terms are retained solely because of their emotional suggestiveness.

Paradox and confusion disappear as soon as it becomes clear that the theory of consciousness is a theory of military relations. It is a theory of military relations among the individuals and social classes of capitalist society which were described by the theory of class structure, but the attributes of these individuals and classes have a purely military significance, since the entire purpose of the theory is to define the path toward the seizure of power by the military general staff. The revolutionary working class, the proletariat, is the army. The virtues of the revolutionary proletariat are exclusively military virtues. Its virtues are not the characteristics which the theory of class structure attributed to *emancipated labor* but the characteristics of a proletariat that *cannot stir, cannot raise itself up,* precisely the characteristics of the proletariat under capitalism. In the theory of class consciousness, the sole virtue of the revolutionary proletariat is *iron discipline while at work with unquestioning obedience to the will of a single person, the leader.* These proletarians are independent and creative to the extent that soldiers are. They are also courageous: their courage is indispensable, since its purpose is *to establish strict, iron discipline backed up by the state power of the armed workers* over the whole of society. To the extent that workers refuse to join this army voluntarily and resist being recruited, they are guilty of *petty-bourgeois spinelessness, disunity, individualism, and alternate moods of exaltation and dejection.* They are *deserters to the bourgeoisie,* deserters to the enemy camp.

Just as the characteristics of the revolutionary army—discipline and obedience—are precisely the characteristics which workers already possess under capitalism, the characteristics of the leaders are precisely the characteristics of leaders in capitalist society. But the leaders of capitalism are the bourgeoisie, the enemy. This difficulty is resolved by means of a sado-masochistic reasoning which aspiring leaders must learn to apply adeptly if they are at all serious. The reasoning begins with the observable fact that, under capitalism, the sole characteristics of the proletariat are discipline and obedience, the characteristics of the soldiers of an army, whereas the bourgeoisie are the planners, coordinators, strategists, in short the decision-makers. Since the characteristics of the vanguard of the proletariat are the ability to plan, coordinate, strategize, in short to make decisions, this vanguard cannot consist of proletarians and must consist of *representatives of the propertied classes, bourgeois intellectuals.* This self-conception of the leaders is degrading, since they see themselves as bedfellows of the hated enemy, the bourgeoisie. But the pain which the leaders thus inflict on themselves is alleviated by the gratifying fact that, by assuming the enemy's attributes they also assume the enemy's powers, the power to order, decree, legislate, and decide, the power to manage and control the subordinates whose sole attribute is their desire to obey. *We must consolidate what we ourselves have won, what we ourselves have decreed, made law, discussed, planned -- consolidate all this in stable forms of everyday labor discipline. This is the most difficult, but the most gratifying task.*

Although the reasoning itself is solidly grounded in capitalist reality, the empirical basis for its propositions is not actually very solid. The characterization of the revolutionary leaders, the vanguard of the proletariat, as representatives of the propertied classes, as bourgeois intellectuals, requires something like a leap of the imagination. In terms of their relation to social means of production, very few of the historical revolutionary leaders have been representatives of the propertied classes, namely bourgeois. Most of them have in fact been unemployed writers and political hacks who lived on the margins of capitalist society. In terms of their relation to social wealth and property they can only be characterized as having been miserable, if not in their own revolutionary eyes, certainly in the eyes of their neighbors. In terms of their relation to productive activity they have been largely unqualified, a characteristic which they undoubtedly shared with the ruling bourgeoisie. But unlike the bourgeoisie, these marginal writers and full-time hacks did not manage or control the production process, even though they aspired to do so after the seizure of State power. Consequently their self-promotion to the status of *bourgeois intellectuals* already under capitalism had to disregard empirical evidence which embarrasingly pointed to their being no more than marginal workers, sub-proletarians. However, the empirical evidence is ultimately irrelevant, since the theory of class consciousness is not empirical but dialectical; its purpose is to communicate the propositions: bourgeois intellectuals are class conscious proletarians, proletarians are bourgeois, dependence is independence, submission is courage, iron discipline is emancipation, unquestioning obedience is freedom, and the seizure of State power by the vanguard of the proletariat is socialist revolution.

The working people who *engage in independent creative activity as makers of history* remain on the banners of revolutionary organizations. We have shown that independent creative activity is not in fact a sufficient or even a necessary condition for the rise to power of a revolutionary organization. We have also shown that the classical theory of revolutionary organization, the theory of class consciousness, does not regard *independent creative activity* of the *working people* as a condition, but rather as an obstacle to the seizure of State power. Why, then, does independent creative activity remain on the banners of revolutionary organizations? If such activity is not a means to the seizure of State power, is it the goal? If the social relations described on the banners of revolutionary organizations are not conditions for the success of revolutionary organizations, are such relations the expected outcome of the success?

Threescore years after the first successful seizure of State power by a revolutionary organization, the goal of the revolutionary organization ceases to be an enigma proclaimed by slogans on banners. The purpose of revolutionary organizations becomes concrete at the historical moment when the first successful revolutionary leader proclaims that *State power has passed into the hands of the organ of the Council of Workers' and Soldiers' Deputies--the*

87

Revolutionary Military Committee, which heads the proletariat and the garrison. Real, concrete historical practice makes the goal elementary, simple and clear. The historical accomplishment defines the way in which the slogans on the banners are realized. History resolves the contradiction between the independent creative activity of the working people and the seizure of State power by the leaders of a revolutionary organization. There is no longer a contradiction between two propositions, but between a proposition and a historical fact. And a proposition cannot contradict a historical fact. From the moment when *State power has passed into the hands of the organ,* propositions, resolutions and programs become nothing more than a verbal *rigmarole.* From the moment when the historical purpose of a revolutionary organization is defined by hard facts, by historical events, revolutionary organizers can let hard facts speak. It is history that speaks. It is to history that they are responsible. It is by history that they are elected. It is history that defines their goal. It is no longer an individual's imaginings, insights or proofs that argue what is to be done, and by whom. It is history itself that makes it elementary, simple and clear *that classes are led by political parties; that political parties are directed by more or less stable groups composed of the most authoritative, influential and experienced members, who are elected to the most responsible positions and are called leaders. All this is elementary. All this is simple and clear. Why replace this by some rigmarole?* Furthermore, after threescore years of successful seizures of State power, this is something *everyone knows.*

The historical goal of revolutionary leaders is not *some rigmarole,* some slogans in a manifesto, some utopia which has never existed. The historically realized goal of the revolutionary organization is not independent creative activity by the population as agents of history. It is decision-making by the leader as head of State. It is *to consolidate what we ourselves have won, what we ourselves have decreed, made law, discussed, planned--consolidate all this in stable forms of everyday labor discipline. This is the most difficult, but the most gratifying task.* The goal and the most gratifying task of the revolutionary leader is to wield State power.

The wielding of State power requires the same preliminary condition as the seizure of State power. The wielding of the estranged power of community requires the renunciation, the estrangement of this power by the individuals who compose the community. The consolidation of State power requires *everyday labor discipline;* it requires a population under the iron sway of the mass psychology of dependence. The most gratifying task of the revolutionary leader requires a population characterized by *iron discipline while at work,* a working population distinguished by *unquestioning obedience to the will of a single person, the leader, while at work.*

The mass psychology of dependence is the means as well as the goal of the revolutionary leader. The means, as well as the goal, is *socialist revolution with people as they are now, with people who cannot dispense with subordination, control and managers.* The historical possibilities of *people as they are now* are precisely what they are now. These possibilities are realized in *stable forms of every-day labor discipline* characterized by *subordination, control and managers.* These possibilities are not discovered by *working people engaged in independent creative activity as makers of history.* The possibilities for making history *with people as they are now* are defined by what leaders can do in a situation of universal powerlessness.

Why, then, do *the working people engaged in independent creative activity as makers of history* remain on the banners of revolutionary organizations? The historical practice of revolutionary organizations answers this question. The historical seizure of State power by revolutionary organizations is the social practice that gives concrete meanings to the slogans on the banners; the seizure of State power becomes the historical form of the activity described by the slogans. Whatever may have been the *rigmarole* at the origin of the revolutionary slogans, the moment when the Leader of the Bolshevik Party becomes Head of State, all the revolutionary slogans become synonyms for the seizure of State power. Historical fact makes it *indisputable for every Bolshevik that proletarian revolutionary power or Bolshevik power--is now one and the same thing.* —The *self government of the producers,* the *dictatorship of the proletariat,* or the dictatorship of *educated representatives of the propertied classes, intellectuals--is now one and the same thing.* The proletariat, the organization, or the leader—is now one and the same thing. When the State is accepted as the equivalent of the community, the leader as the equivalent of the people, a single individual can speak and decide for the entire community. Although the self-powers of individuals cannot be concentrated in one individual, the estranged powers can be. This follows from the theory of class consciousness. The class and the Party, the people and the leader, are one and the same thing because the Party is the consciousness of the class, the leader is the consciousness of the people. The leader is the mind and spirit, the head—eyes, ears and voice—of the population. The leader's consciousness is the people's consciousness. What the leader decides, the proletariat decides. The seizure of the State apparatus gives the leader the power to make all decisions independently and creatively, the power to make history. This decision-making power in the hands of the leader is the historical form in which *the working people engage in independent creative activity as makers of history.* Since the leader and the Party are the consciousness, the head, the essence of the working class, since the Party and the class *is now one and the same thing,* the advancement of the Party is the same as the advancement of the class.

Independent creative activity is neither the goal nor the means to the seizure of State power. The seizure of power by the leader is realized under the banner of independent creative activity. The historical accomplishment of revolutionary organizations consists of ideological rejection combined with practical realization of the dominant social relations. Revolutionary leaders *must learn to combine the 'public meeting' democracy of the working people--turbulent, surging, overflowing its banks like a spring flood--with the iron discipline while at work, with unquestioning obedience to the will of a single person, the leader, while at work.*

It is only when the goal becomes *elementary, simple, and clear* that the means to this goal can be defined with accuracy and precision. Since the seizure of State power by the revolutionary organization is the historical form of revolution, all means which lead to this goal are by definition revolutionary. A historical *turning point when the vacillations in the ranks of the weak, half-hearted and irresolute-- are strongest,* is a revolutionary situation. *People who cannot dispense with subordination, control and managers* are a revolutionary mass base. The theory of class consciousness helps revolutionary leaders recognize a revolutionary situation in order to derive power out of it; it helps revolutionary leaders recognize a potential revolutionary mass base in order to establish leadership and control over it.

A potentially revolutionary mass base consists of people whose revolutionary consciousness can be raised. The central characteristic of the potential revolutionary does not reside in a propensity to think independently, but in a propensity to think the thoughts of the revolutionary organization and its leaders. In fact, the less prone the individual is to independent thought and action and the more likely the individual is to follow the lead of the organization, the higher the individual's revolutionary potential. In short, potential followers are potential revolutionaries. The revolutionary potential of the proletariat depends on workers' willingness to follow the revolutionary organization *with iron discipline and unquestioning obedience.*

The theory of class consciousness serves aspiring leaders as an instrument for locating potential revolutionaries, potential objects for consciousness-raising. A potential revolutionary is characterized by material oppression combined with a lack of consciousness. Such an individual unconsciously experiences the material oppression as unbearable, but does not know that what is missing is revolutionary leadership. The individual's mind is a *tabula rasa* on which the thoughts of revolutionary leaders are to be inscribed. When this individual becomes conscious of the indispensability of subordination to the revolutionary organization and control by the revolutionary leader, the individual becomes a conscious revolutionary.

Working people in industrially developed capitalist regions have not been ideal objects for consciousness-raising historically. Although they have on numerous occasions tried to destroy the capitalist shell in which their productive activity is contained, they have not historically demonstrated the *iron discipline and unquestioning obedience* of a *revolutionary proletariat* as defined by the theory of class consciousness. To the extent that they have moved to reappropriate their self-powers, they have moved independently and creatively, dispensing with *subordination, control and managers.* They have not been characterized by a propensity to follow revolutionary leaders. This is why the theory of class consciousness characterizes such workers as *privileged,* as a *labor aristocracy,* as a *bourgeois proletariat alongside the bourgeoisie. The distinguishing characteristic of the theory of the labor aristocracy* is that, from its standpoint, *the industrial workers in the metropoles of imperialism are not merely prisoners of bourgeois ideology; they have deserted to the bourgeoisie.* Due to their relation to highly developed productive forces, these working people have achieved some degree of independence. This independence is what marks them as being aristocratic, bourgeois and privileged, because the independence is manifested in an unwillingness to follow the lead of the *bourgeois intellectuals* who are the vanguard of the proletariat.

The theory of class consciousness does not abandon the standpoint of the revolutionary leader; *it proceeds to answer the fundamental strategic questions, who are our friends and who are our enemies, from that standpoint.* It locates the friends of revolutionary leaders among *the people in countries oppressed by imperialism.* The more oppressed these people are, the more removed from highly developed productive forces, the less likely they are to have achieved any degree of independence. In short, the more oppressed, the less privileged. And the less privileged, the more likely to become friends of revolutionary leaders. If their situation makes them helpless in the face of contemporary productive forces, this helplessness is not a disease to be cured by independent creative practice; it is the sign of their revolutionary potential.

The revolutionary potential of the oppressed, as defined by the theory of class consciousness, is directly proportional to their level of dependence. The more people are subordinated and controlled, and the less they can dispense with subordination and control, the higher their revolutionary potential. This is why *the people in countries oppressed by imperialism* have been a virtual cornucopia for revolutionary leaders. Submission to revolutionary leaders has made the oppressed the vanguard of the proletariat. And the leaders who have built power out of the ghettos, power out of the "native" quarters, power out of the frustrations and resentments, power out of the killings—leaders who, according to the same theory of class consciousness, *themselves belonged to the bourgeois intelligentsia*—have been the vanguard of the vanguard.

The situation of the people in countries oppressed by imperialism has been the historical field out of which revolutionary organizations and leaders built power. This is the field which contained the necessary as well as the sufficient conditions for the seizure of State power by revolutionary organizations. Modern revolutionary theory treats the oppressed as potential revolutionaries by definition. The oppressed become conscious revolutionaries when their actions increase the power of the revolutionary Party. Those whose actions hamper the Party are by definition privileged. And those who superficially seem to be oppressed, but whose practice gives no evidence of revolutionary consciousness, are defined as lackeys of imperialism. On the basis of this elementary, simple and clear definition of the social classes in the modern world, it has been possible to define the fundamental contradiction of modern capitalism as the conflict between oppressed and oppressor nations. Within oppressor nations, aspiring revolutionary leaders have focussed their attention on people who could, in one or another respect, be plausibly treated as an oppressed nation.

Oppressed nations are the revolutionary proletariat in modern revolutionary theory. They are oppressed, not because they reproduce the dominant productive forces of the ruling social order, but to the extent that they do not. They are potential revolutionaries, not because their daily activity requires independent creative acts which burst the bounds of the dominant social order, but because it does not. The proletariat of modern revolutionary theory is not located at the heart of capitalism, but at its margins. The oppressed are revolutionary proletarians, not in terms of their relation to the dominant productive forces of capitalism, but in terms of their relation to the dominant revolutionary organizations. The material situation of the oppressed is one which is expected to make them disciplined and obedient followers. It is a material situation whose known consequence has not been independent and creative decision-making, but the mass psychology of dependence. It is a situation characterized, not by the omnipresence of the productive forces which are estranged by producers in the social form of Capital, but by the general absence of such productive forces. It is the situation of people who do not yet fully engage in modern forms of social activity, who do not yet wield the dominant forms of social power represented by money and State offices. The revolutionary potential of the oppressed lies in the willingness to support, at least passively, the struggle for power of a social class whose known historical role has been to spread the modern forms of reproducing Capital. This revolutionary potential cannot take the form of independent creative activity in conditions where the material basis for the independence and creativity possible to contemporary human beings is largely missing. The revolutionary potential takes the form of a desire for the amenities available to human beings in fully developed capitalist regions. The oppressed, who do not themselves produce such amenities, imagine these products, not as products of labor, but as products of the social form of the developed capitalist regions. The oppressed are under the impression that it is the social form that creates these amenities. And it is precisely this social form that the revolutionary organization is able to provide.

The theory of the fundamental contradiction of modern capitalism, also known as the theory of imperialism, is the clearest and most succinct statement of the modern theory of revolutionary leadership. This theory adapts the classical theory of social classes to the requirements of modern revolutionary leaders. The classical theory had dealt with a system of social relations through which one individual, a producer, systematically alienated productive activity, while another individual, a capitalist, systematically appropriated the alienated activity as well as all its products. Whether or not the producer and the exploiter spoke the same language was not relevant in the classical theory, although in general they did. On the other hand, the modern theory of the fundamental contradiction does not deal with social relations among the individuals of a society, but with international relations, with relations between countries. The adaptation of the classical theory to the needs of revolutionary leaders begins by shifting the frame of reference: *In order to understand the relations between classes within a given country, it is necessary to understand also the relationship of that country to other countries within the entire production sphere. An analysis of class relations requires an analysis of international relations.* The analysis of international relations leads to the discovery that, unlike the *privileged bourgeois proletariat* of oppressor nations which alienates its labor to capitalists who speak the same language, the oppressed alienate their labor to foreign capitalists. As a result, economic development, namely the process of accumulation of Capital, does not take place in the oppressed nations; it is exported to oppressor nations. The solution to this fundamental contradiction is national liberation. The nation is liberated when its resources and productive forces are nationalized, when the nation's productive activity is appropriated and directed by the Party of National Liberation and the National Leader. The modern theory stands the classical theory on its head. According to the modern theory, the fundamental contradiction, the central illness of the oppressed, is not capitalism; it is the absence of national capitalism. What ails the oppressed is the absence of modern forms of *subordination, control and managers.* The fundamental crisis of the oppressed is the crisis of leadership. The fundamental question for the oppressed is the question of State power. The illness of the oppressed is diagnosed in such a way that the cure is self-evident. The cure is modern forms of *subordination, control and managers.* The cure is the national leader at the helm of the State.

It has long been known that a very large number of the human beings who sacrifice their limbs and their lives to national liberation struggles, the populations who make up the *mass base* of the liberation army, sacrifice themselves to achieve *the self government of the producers,* to *engage in independent creative activity as makers of history.* When national leaders seize State power, these populations are rewarded with the prevailing modern forms of *self-government* and *independence.* Self-government takes the form of government by rulers who speak the national language. Independence takes the form of National Independence, government by the National Leader.

As a result of the seizure of State power by a revolutionary leader, populations who struggle for independent creative activity by self-governed producers achieve *a socialist society governed by a dictatorship of the proletariat led by the Workers' Party which follows a unitary ideology composed exclusively of the ideas of the party secretary-general based on the creative application of Marxism-Leninism.* As a result of the seizure of State power, the leader personifies all the resources, all the productive forces and all the activity of the society. Personifications of social activity animate the world. Estranged power of community—the State—is experienced as the only real community. Estranged productive power—Capital—is experienced as the only real productive agent. The leader personifies the entirety of social Capital. *Whatever we have, all we have built, is entirely owing to the correct leadership of comrade party secretary-general. The Premier's ideas form the basis for what we call the unitary ideology espoused by the Workers' Party. Unitary ideology means there are no contending ideologies. The unitary ideology of the system of the party means the adoption, as the sole guiding principle, of the revolutionary ideas of comrade party secretary-general, founder and leader of the party and great leader of the revolution. The leader founds and leads the party which is the vanguard of the working class and the general staff of the revolution. He is the supreme brain of the class and the heart of the party who puts forward the guiding ideas of the party as well as the strategy and tactics of the revolution. He is the center of the unity and solidarity of the working class and the entire revolutionary masses. There is no center except him. It is an indispensable need in leading socialism and communism to a final triumph to resolutely defend the leader of the revolution and form a steel-like ring around him to strictly protect and carry out his revolutionary ideas.*

The historical achievement of revolutionary leaders who seized power has been to liberate the nation's raw materials and the nation's labor force from the imperialists, namely foreign capitalists, in order to launch an epoch of primitive accumulation of Capital by the State. The oppressed who were mobilized into the *mass base* that put the vanguard in power have served as the sources of the accumulated Capital. The social relations which accompanied this process had to be social relations which responded to the historical task of primitive accumulation of Capital. The historical achievement of successful revolutionary leaders has been to *organize large scale production on the basis of what capitalism has already created, establishing strict, iron discipline backed up by the state power of the armed workers.* Anti-imperialist revolution has been the modern means for launching and completing the accumulation of Capital in regions which had been left stranded by the main historical trend. The historical mission of socialist revolutions has been to complete the dominant social order in space and in depth.

The historical realization of economic development, namely accumulation of Capital, involves the transfer of surplus labor from agrarian to industrial regions, from productive classes to exempted classes. It entails the unequal development of geographic and social sectors; the social and economic development of some at the expense of others. The accumulation of Capital requires and thus gives rise to social relations which lubricate and enforce it. These social relations have taken the historical form of the State, commodity production and the division of labor.

Because the accumulation of Capital began in Western Europe, and its initial agency appeared in the form of a commercial bourgeoisie, apologists for this class credited the accumulation of Capital to the institutions and ideas of this specific class. It was thought that Capital depended on entrepreneurial merchants attached to democratic political forms, an anti-religious ideology of science and enlightenment, and a social program of universal literacy. However, the launching of the primitive accumulation of Capital in Japan after 1868 demonstrated that the process could dispense with the West European bourgeoisie and with its liberal-democratic ideology. Japanese industrialization demonstrated that the social relations required for the primitive accumulation of Capital are a strong State, universal commodity production, and the division of labor. The remaining institutions and ideas of the West European bourgeoisie were not requirements of Capital accumulation; they reflected the peculiar historical origins of the European bourgeoisie. Japanese industrialization demonstrated that democratic political forms were not a requirement of Capital accumulation but a reflection of the bourgeoisie's struggle against feudalism. Japanese industrialization demonstrated that the anti-religious scientific ideology of the West European bourgeoisie was not a requirement of Capital accumulation but a reflection of the bourgeoisie's struggle against the anti-commercial ideology of the Catholic Church. Japanese industrialization demonstrated that the bourgeois program of universal literacy and humanist education was not a requirement of Capital accumulation but a reflection of the bourgeoisie's struggle against the obscurantism of Christianity. The fact is that the West European bourgeoisie itself abandoned its own initial institutions and ideas because they hampered the accumulation of Capital. Democracy undermined the authority of the State, and so the bourgeoisie detached the democratic forms from the exercise of sovereignty and reduced them to socially harmless rituals. The anti-religious ideology of science and elightenment hampered commodity production by removing the moral justification for the sacrifice of an individual's productive life to the service of a higher community, so the bourgeoisie resurrected religion. Universal literacy undermined the division of labor by making all branches of human knowledge available to all, so the bourgeoisie transformed literacy into an instrument for the mass production of historically unprecedented forms of ignorance.

The Bolshevik seizure of State power in 1917 confirmed the lessons learned from the Japanese restoration of the centralized State in 1868. The accumulation of Capital can dispense with the institutions and ideas of the West European bourgeoisie; what is required is the State, commodity production and the division of labor. Bourgeois democratic forms no longer hamper the authority of the State even as rituals; they have been replaced by a State which represents and embodies the entire population. The anti-religious ideology no longer hampers commodity production; labor is once again a painful sacrifice suffered for the glory of a higher community. Universal literacy no longer undermines the division of labor; it has become an instrument for inculcating reverence for the State, belief in the official ideology, and *iron discipline while at work.*

The historical accomplishment of seizures of State power by revolutionary organizations has been to spread the relations of Capital accumulation to regions where these relations were underdeveloped. This historical accomplishment has been carried out without the ideology of the West European bourgeoisie. The West European bourgeoisie had initiated the primitive accumulation of Capital with an ideology that reflected the historical origin of this class. Revolutionary organizations that seize power initiate the primitive accumulation of Capital with an ideology that reflects the historical origin of modern revolutionary organizations. Modern revolutionary ideology does not borrow its language from the West European bourgeoisie but from the West European working class. This ideology refers to the historical practice of primitive accumulation of Capital with the language of socialism. The language of socialism did not originate in regions where the social relations of Capital accumulation were underdeveloped. It originated in regions where the relations of Capital accumulation were most highly developed. The language of socialism originally expressed a total rejection of the social relations of Capital accumulation. It originally expressed an unmitigated opposition to *subordination, control and managers,* to *iron discipline and unquestioning obedience.* It was not originally a theory of the seizure of power by revolutionary leaders. Its original frame of reference was unambiguous: *Let it come to an end at last, this great scandal that our posterity will never believe! Disappear at last, revolting distinctions between rich and poor, great and small, masters and servants, governors and governed.* In the frame of reference of the original language of socialism, the social relations of Capital accumulation stunt the capacities of individuals. The universal reappropriation of every individual's capacities is therefore the *sine qua non* for socialism. The word socialism does not originally refer to a state of affairs; it is a negation of the prevailing state of affairs. The word socialism is originally a synonym for what never before existed. It is originally a synonym for the unrealized potentialities of society's productive forces, a synonym for the undeveloped capacities of human beings. It is originally a synonym for the overthrow of the social order that blocks the potentialities and stunts the capacities. It is originally a synonym for the universal development of human capacities to the level made possible by the productive forces.

Seizures of State power were achieved by revolutionary leaders in conditions characterized by a low level of development of productive forces. The historical role of the revolutionary States was to develop the productive forces by instituting relations of Capital accumulation. The unrealized potentialities of the productive forces that were realized were potentialities that had not been realized locally. The seizure of State power paved the way for the universal development of the capacities of the State to the level made possible by contemporary productive forces.

The bourgeois program of democracy, enlightenment and universal literacy did not become completely serviceable to the bourgeoisie's historical task until it was emptied of its original content and transformed into an ideology of Capital accumulation and State power. The socialist program inherited by modern revolutionary leaders speaks of workers' democracy, appropriation of productive activity by each, development of universal capacities—namely of the abolition of the State, commodity production, and the division of labor. This program is even less serviceable to the social relations established by the seizure of State power than the bourgeois program. But the socialist language could not be rejected because it is only this language that makes the seizure of power by revolutionary leaders *a revolutionary alternative in the heart of the empire.* Consequently, the language of socialism had to be completely emptied of its original content to be transformed into an ideology of Capital accumulation and State power. The transformation of socialist language into a vehicle for communicating the accumulation of Capital and the seizure of State power has been the major feat of modern revolutionary leaders. In the transformed language, the State, which had originally been a synonym for the alienation of community, becomes a synonym for the community. Commodity production, originally a synonym for alienated productive activity, becomes a synonym for the construction of socialism. The division of labor, originally a synonym for the alienation of universal human capacities, becomes a synonym for the realization of human capacities, and the specialist becomes the new socialist man.

The unique historical feat of V.I. Lenin was not to seize State power; this had been done before. Lenin's historical feat was to describe his seizure of State power with the language of a socialist movement determined to destroy the State. The application of Lenin's ideas to Lenin's practice is the foundation for modern revolutionary ideology. For aspiring leaders armed with revolutionary ideas, the revolutionary ideology provides a vision of the social power historically achieved by leaders armed with revolutionary ideas. For individuals who are removed from contact with modern productive forces by the division of labor, whose only developed capacities are their revolutionary ideas, the revolutionary ideology provides a vision of total self-realization.

The revolutionary ideology refers to a historical state of affairs. It is not a negation but an affirmation. It is a description of the realized potentialities of modern productive forces. The revolutionary ideology describes the only modern social form in which all of society's productive forces are directly at the disposal of the leader who heads the State. The revolutionary leader is the modern Prince. This is why it is urgent for aspiring leaders to understand the historical conditions which may lead them to a future which is available only to a single individual in any given period. The revolutionary ideology describes the conditions for the seizure, consolidation and maintenance of State power in the words of revolutionary leaders who seized State power. Modern revolutionary ideology consists of the autobiographies of successful revolutionary leaders. *The ideas of the ruling* revolutionary leaders *are the ruling* revolutionary *ideas.* The revolutionary leaders who become *the ruling material force* of the society in which they seize State power are *at the same time its ruling intellectual force.* Revolutionary leaders who have *the means of material production* at their disposal have *control at the same time over the means of mental production, so that thereby, generally speaking, the ideas of those who lack the means of mental production are subject* to the ideas of the successful revolutionaries. *The ruling* revolutionary *ideas are nothing* less *than the ideal expression of the material relationships* at the base of the revolutionary State, *the material relationships grasped as ideas; hence of the relationships which make* these leaders rulers, *therefore, the ideas of* their rule.

The fact that the revolutionary ideology consists of the ideas of revolutionary rulers about their own rule carries certain dangers of self-exposure. The ideology raises the consciousness of aspiring leaders, but it also raises the consciousness of individuals who do not aspire to State power. This danger is alleviated first of all by the historical law that no social form is definitively discarded before all its possibilities have been exhausted. At present the seizure of State power by revolutionary leaders has only been realized in half the world. (The other half continues to be ruled by the historical remnants of a capitalist class which has in fact merged with the State, but which has failed to develop an ideology that adequately articulates the total reconciliation of this class with its one-time archenemy.) Secondly, the danger of self-exposure is alleviated by the language in which the revolutionary ideology is communicated. Every statement is simultaneously an invocation and an instruction. For the potential follower the language invokes the historical moment when the working class takes power, a situation in which all individuals regain their estranged self-powers. To achieve this end, followers are instructed to do what other revolutionaries did: support the leader. The same statement defines the next move of the leader, but it does not inform the follower of the move of the leader. The phrases of the revolutionary ideology are understood differently, they have different meanings, for leaders and for followers.

The power to communicate double meanings was produced by the historical development of the modern revolutionary ideology. The socialist origin of the language is retained in the semantics of the revolutionary ideology, in the conventionally accepted meanings of the words. This socialist language does not directly refer to leaders or to aspirants to leadership; it refers to producers, and specifically to their reappropriation of the powers they estrange to Capital and the State. These semantic meanings are today reserved for followers. For leaders the language has an entirely different meaning, based on the *historical experience of the revolutionary socialist movement.* This historical experience is the seizure of State power by revolutionary leaders. A language which expressed collective determination to reappropriate estranged power has become an instrument for communicating the seizure of State power. The language of the withering away of the State has become the official ideology of the State. The original meanings of the socialist words are not discarded. On the contrary, the power of modern revolutionary ideology resides in the fact that the original meanings are scrupulously retained. Self-activity, independence and freedom, Marxism, socialism and communism, the dictatorship of the proletariat and even the withering away of the State have all become vehicles for the expression of double meanings. Each term simultaneously evokes a specific phenomenon and also its opposite. Each term refers simultaneously to a universal and a particular, a plural and a singular, many and one, the people and the leader, the community and the State. Each term simultaneously communicates a thesis and its negation. The power to communicate two contradictory thoughts with the same words is what makes this ideology dialectical. When the thesis and its negation are both communicated by the same term, the two become One; they fuse; the negation becomes the embodiment of the thesis. Thus the rule of the leader is not a means to the rule of all, nor is it a symbol of the rule of all. The rule of the leader IS the rule of all. The two are one. The dialectical revolutionary ideology stands bourgeois logic on its head.

Workers control production when they seize State power. This follows from the *historical experience of the revolutionary socialist movement.* But workers can seize State power only when leaders seize State power. This follows from the definition of the State. Therefore workers control production when leaders seize State power. The seizure of State power by the leaders is not a means to workers' control of production; it IS workers' control. The two are one. The invocation of double thoughts is the key to revolutionary leadership and the heart of the historical experience of the revolutionary socialist movement.

In spite of the historical achievements of revolutionary organizations, this model of activity seems to be discredited among the working populations of already industrialized regions. One would think that repeated failure would discredit a model of social activity. One would not expect a history of repeated successes to contribute to the possibility of failure. But aspiring leaders should be warned that this is precisely the case. The possibility of failure is a direct result of the historical successes of the revolutionary model. These successes have been broadcast to every corner of the globe by increasingly universal means of communication. As a result of this publicity, all potential constituents, all potential members and followers of the revolutionary organization, including the poorest and most oppressed, are relatively well informed about the aims and purposes of a revolutionary vanguard.

One would think that the possibility of failure is created by the unfavorable publicity given to revolutionary organizations by capitalist propaganda. But a closer look at this publicity reveals that this is not the case. The capitalist establishment, the owners of means of production and mass media of communication, do broadcast publicity unfavorable to revolutionary organizations and leaders. Publicity experts describe communism and revolution in ways that are expected to serve the interests of the experts' employers. Communists are depicted as enemies of culture, religion, and all the values of society. But the result of this publicity is not what the experts are paid for. Working people who have no great love for their exploiters and fewer illusions are shown that communists are enemies of their exploiters, enemies of capitalist culture, religion and all the values of the ruling society—namely that communists are champions of freedom. The effect of capitalist publicity is to make large numbers of people sympathetic to communists.

The effects of capitalist publicity are in fact negated by revolutionary propaganda. Revolutionary theorists publicize the successes of the victorious vanguards who seized power over the State, the means of production and the mass media of communication. They design this information in ways that are expected to serve the interests of the vanguard at the helm of the revolutionary State. The revolutionary propaganda points to the victories of the revolutionary State in all realms of human activity. It points to the successes of the revolutionary State in raising the consciousness of all the people, especially the consciousness of sectors of the population whose lack of sympathy for the Dictatorship of the Proletariat had made them *prisoners of bourgeois ideology.* During the years immediately following the seizure of power, revolutionary propaganda concentrates on the economic victories of the Socialist State. This is because the early social victories do not provide much material for favorable publicity. However, during later years, a more comprehensive picture of the Socialist State is drawn. This is because the significance of the economic victories diminishes due to unforeseen obstacles to economic development—obstacles which in some instances have created negative rates of economic development. Consequently, the narrowly economic approach is replaced by a more universal approach. Propaganda turns to the victories of the Socialist State in realms of national engineering, national science, and the people's arts. It depicts the victories scored in the area of psychology, particularly the applications of this science to problems of revolutionary consciousness, counter-revolutionary elements, and correct thought.

The revolutionary propaganda and the capitalist propaganda contradict each other on every point. But the result of the contradiction is not what the propagandists intend to achieve. This suggests that the sciences of psychology and mass communication are both in their infancy and still have much to learn. The effect of the revolutionary propaganda is not to create enthusiasm for the historical achievements of the Socialist State, but to create the phenomenon known in revolutionary literature as "anti-communist hysteria." As a result of the revolutionary propaganda, potential constituents of the revolutionary organization, including the most oppressed, do not greet revolutionary leaders as liberators but as manipulators and oppressors. Despite, or rather because of half a century of victorious construction of Socialism in half the world, revolutionary leaders encounter a profound rank and file hostility to the revolutionary seizure of power. Despite, or rather because of half a century of revolutionary propaganda, aspiring leaders encounter a lower level of revolutionary consciousness than was know to exist before this half-century of socialist victories began.

The fact that working people have in general become hostile to revolutionary organizers does not indicate that they no longer struggle for *the self government of the producers.* The low level of consciousness of contemporary working people does not indicate that they no longer attempt to *engage in independent creative activity as makers of history.* Their hostility and their consciousness indicate that they are unwilling to struggle for the forms of self-government and independence historically achieved by revolutionary seizures of

101

State power. Their lack of revolutionary consciousness, namely their unwillingness to follow revolutionary leaders, does not indicate that they are no longer subject to the mass psychology of dependence. If that were the case, the capitalist as well as the socialist *superincumbent strata of official society* would already have been *sprung into the air.* Struggles for independent creative activity are still curtailed by *vacillation,* by lack of confidence, by anxiety in the face of the unknown. But few seem convinced that the social practice which would conquer the anxiety is the historical practice of revolutionary leaders. Very few working individuals appear to believe that the experience in which they lack self-confidence is the *historical experience of the world socialist movement.*

Revolutionary leaders need *people who cannot dispense with subordination, control and managers* in order to establish *strict iron discipline backed up by the state power of the armed workers.* But *armed workers* can dispense with subordination, control, managers, iron discipline and State power. Armed workers have not demonstrated their understanding of the revolutionary insight that what they need to make their lives complete is a revolutionary leader. In fact, struggles for independent creative activity have increasingly dispensed with revolutionary leaders. Vacillation and anxiety in the face of the unknown have been gripping the revolutionary leaders. In struggles for independent creative activity, revolutionary leaders increasingly find themselves asking for help in a world unfamiliar to them. And even when the struggles for independence lose their impetus and halt only one small step further than previous struggles, they do not in their decline set the stage for the seizure of State power by revolutionary leaders. Failures to achieve *the self-government of the producers* have not paved the way for self-government by the leaders. On the contrary, populations that failed to achieve independence have preferred to step back to the dominant social order. They already know what the ruling State will grant. They also know how to get what it can grant. They do not know what the revolutionary State will grant, and they do not know if there are ways to get it. As a result, organizers armed with the ideas of revolutionary rulers have become increasingly isolated. They are becoming less and less able to reproduce *the historical experience of the world socialist movement.* After half a century of scientific construction of Socialism, the modern revolutionary organizer finds it increasingly difficult to raise the consciousness of a potential constituent who considers the future leader a manipulator, liar, and future cop. This difficulty creates the possibility that the time for the seizure of State power may be over, that the most careful attempts to seize the time may fail.

Revolutionary leaders may fail to establish power over struggles for *independent creative activity.* Does this mean that the age of revolutionary leadership is over? By no means. It merely means that aspiring revolutionary leaders would be well advised to look for power elsewhere. It means that aspiring leaders would do well to locate alternative sources of power. Such alternatives are plainly visible, and latter-day revolutionary leaders have not hesitated to seize them. But a slavish attachment to revolutionary orthodoxy has kept aspiring leaders from exploiting these alternatives fully.

Inflexible devotion to *the initiative of millions, creating a democracy on their own, in their own way,* can lead to nothing but failure for revolutionary leaders. The *independent creative activity* of millions promises nothing more than extinction for revolutionary organizers. Independent activity is neither the means to the seizure of State power nor its goal. The means as well as the goal were defined by the *historical experience of the world socialist movement.* This historical experience has made it clear that the social relations behind revolutionary consciousness are the conditions for revolutionary leadership, and State power is the goal. These social relations are dependence relations. Dependence relations are a normal part of daily life in contemporary societies. They are a constant source of power for revolutionary leaders. Struggles for independence do not give rise to dependence relations; they put an end to them. Consequently there is absolutely no reason for aspiring leaders to wait for the masses to come knocking at their doors. The masses are not likely to come during normal times because they already have leaders; they are even less likely to come during struggles for independence when they attempt to dispense with leaders. If revolutionary leadership is not to become extinct, leaders cannot remain inflexibly devoted to *bursts of creative enthusiasm* which hold nothing in store for them. The alternative for revolutionary leaders is to exploit all the conditions for revolutionary leadership provided by modern society, to inject revolutionary ideology and leadership into all the normal activities of capitalist daily life.

A class conscious mass base is the solid rock on which a leader's power rests. Mass acceptance of the leader is the proof of the class's consciousness. The larger the mass under the hegemony of a revolutionary leader, the greater the revolutionary consciousness of the class. Every increment in the leader's power signifies an increase in the revolutionary consciousness of the class. All means to increase the leader's power are means to raise the consciousness of the class. Therefore all means to increase the leader's power are revolutionary means. The conditions described by classical revolutionary theory— *the initiative of millions, independent creative activity*—are not revolutionary means. Anxiety in the face of the unknown, *vacillation in the ranks of the weak,* are revolutionary means. But they are not the only means. Revolutionary leaders can no longer afford to over-look any of the means in the capitalist arsenal. Whatever advances the bearers of revolutionary consciousness is a revolutionary instrument.

Conditions for the establishment of revolutionary leadership are part of the fabric of capitalist social life. Intelligent use of these conditions requires behavior identical to that required for the seizure of the State apparatus. If the degree of sacrifice were the sole measure of a leader's revolutionary aspirations, then nothing short of the absolute seizure of the State apparatus could live up to the leader's expectations. But one cannot take into account only sub-jective factors. One must also recognize objective circumstances. And objective circumstances may be such that the absolute seizure of State power is not immediately realizable. Aspiring leaders may have to absolve their lives by establishing forms of power which, though they appear less total, are identical to the seizure of the State apparatus in terms of their consequences. There is no need to regard alternative forms of power as less rewarding than the *sole duty of a revolutionary.* In view of the single-minded devotion and self-sacrifice that characterize a revolutionary leader's lifelong struggle, there is no need to designate the available alternatives as *one step forward, two steps back.* The classical language of dialectical materialism gives revolutionary leaders a method with which to depict the available alternatives much more dialectically, namely positively. The first step toward the re-evaluation of the contemporary situation of revolu-tionary leaders is to realize publicly, namely in such a way as to make constituents realize, that the great revolutionary leaders of this century were not dogmatic. The great revolutionary leaders were not Talmudists. Their relation to the revolutionary ideology was not wooden, it was not inflexible. The dialectical materialism of the great leaders has nothing in common with bourgeois rigidity. The great revolutionary leaders were above all great dialecticians. They re-cognized that the negation of the negation always led to a new and higher level. In the style of the great revolutionary dialecticians, and in view of available alternatives, the aspiring leader may reason as follows: In case of the negation, or temporary postponement, of the victory of the revolutionary ideology which represented the first negation, the task of the revolutionary is to negate the second negation by raising the ideology to a qualitatively higher level of struggle. Since the negation of the victory is due to objective circum-stances, to the imperialist last stage of capitalism which was negated by anti-imperialist ideology in the first instance, the revolutionary leader must adapt the tactics of the struggle to the changed circum-stances. The leader must make it clear to his constituents that, in a period of ideological struggle, one who fails to adapt the revolu-tionary coherence of the ideology to the historical circumstances of the class struggle has not learned to use the materialist dialectic in a correct revolutionary manner and would do well to study this subject in the appropriate classics.

Steps which prepare for and lead to the establishment of power by a revolutionary leader constitute revolutionary movement. At every step the revolutionary consciousness of the class is raised. The revolutionary task is to raise the consciousness of as many as possible, to establish the power of the leader over as many as possible. The task of the revolutionary organization is to create the conditions for socialist revolution, to lay the ground for the Dictatorship of the Proletariat, to establish the power of the revolutionary organization, to build the revolutionary establishment. The revolutionary establishment consists of *the most authoritative, influential and experienced.* The revolutionary establishment consists of workers and staff members, followers and leaders. The staff members, or leaders, are individuals who are able to be conscious full time because their daily activity separates them from the social means of production, because they do not have daily contact with society's productive forces. The staff members may be artists, independent professionals, full time political organizers, and particularly politicians and academics. If the revolutionary establishment is the vanguard of the proletariat, these revolutionary intellectuals are the vanguard of the establishment. The staff members are the repositories of the revolutionary ideology. They embody the revolutionary consciousness of the working class. They are the thought of the proletariat. These intellectuals are the spearhead of the revolutionary movement. Although New Left intellectuals differ about premises and about conclusions, they are unified by one element: methodology. The methodology that unites them is dialectical materialism. Dialectical materialism is a term coined by F. Engels which was elaborated into a complete science by V.I. Lenin. The specific purpose of this science is to determine the laws governing the seizure of State power by the vanguard of the proletariat. Class consciousness, the negation of capitalism, is the key concept of the science. Class consciousness is the essence of the working class: it is what makes this class the living negation of capitalism. Revolutionary intellectuals are the bearers of class consciousness. The revolutionary establishment is the only expression of the revolutionary essence of the class. And the revolutionary leaders are the living embodiment of this essence. Revolutionary intellectuals are thus the key agents of change, the makers of history. Dialectical materialism scientifically determines that the staff members of the revolutionary establishment, also known as the cadre, are the spearhead of history. But this does not mean that every staff member is a spearhead. Revolutionary class consciousness is unitary. It is not many thoughts about many things, but a single thought about what is to be done. Each revolutionary intellectual cannot develop class consciousness on his or her own. There is only one correct strategy, one correct theory, one correct ideology. Correct revolutionary consciousness is not the thought of this individual today and that individual tomorrow. It is the thought of the leader of the world's working class yesterday, today and tomorrow. *Every movement of world importance exists only in the head of some chosen being, and the fate of the world depends on whether this head is or is not mortally wounded by some realistic stone before it has had time to make its revelation. The whole historical development consists of those theoretical abstractions which originate in the heads of all the philosophers and ideologists of the age, and since it is impossible to put all these heads together and induce them to "take counsel and register their votes," there must of necessity be one* central *head, the spearhead of all these philosophical and ideological heads, in a word, the speculative unity of all these* staff members—the Leader.

The revolutionary establishment consists of relations of mutual dependence between the revolutionary staff members, or organizers, and their constituents. The organizers depend on the constituents for their power. The constituents depend on the organizers for their consciousness. In other words, a progressive division of mental and manual labor characterizes the revolutionary establishment. It is the specific task of the organizers to channel the undirected acts of their constituents into the tried and tested paths defined by the ideology and confirmed by the revolutionary experience of the world socialist movement.

Since the thought of the revolutionary leader is the essence of the working class and the key agent of history, the central problem of modern capitalism is the general absence of this thought. This absence of revolutionary consciousness characterizes labor unions, communities, professions, academies and the government itself. The absence of revolutionary leaders with anti-imperialist ideology is particularly critical in the labor unions. Without revolutionary leadership, the unions are not used to educate the workers, to implant a unitary ideology, iron discipline and unquestioning obedience to the will of the leader. *The problem of the unions, however, lies not with the workers, but with the political philosophy of social democracy. By refusing to ideologically attack capitalism as a system, the union remains with a piecemeal approach, attempting to reduce issues to technical considerations thereby confusing its membership, not educating them.* Establishment of revolutionary leadership over the unions would put an end to the political philosophy of social democracy, the piecemeal approach and the technical considerations. Revolutionary leadership over the unions would eliminate the 'anticommunist hysteria' of the working class, since it would make revolutionary leaders important, legitimate and respectable forces in the democratic political life of the country. Revolutionary labor leaders would not be mere brokers who sell workers for the sake of the highest available wage; they would be brokers who would sell workers for the sake of anti-imperialism and socialism. In this sense, revolutionary labor leaders would officially represent the negation of capitalist social relations.

Labor unions are important. But they are only one source of power for revolutionary leaders. Victims of capitalist repression are another source of power. Ideologically correct treatment of the fear of repression can transform this fear into a powerful instrument for the establishment of revolutionary leadership. This fear has been successfully used by revolutionary leaders in numerous ways. For example, aspiring leaders have taken temporary residence in communities where police harassment is frequent. By provoking the police, the aspiring leader secured his own arrest as well as the arrest of several members of the community. The leader's friends then organized repression conferences and campaigns to 'Free the Revolutionary 10,' on all occasions emphasizing the anti-imperialist ideology of the leader. The initial supporters of the conferences and campaigns are the relatives and friends of the arrested community members. Initially gathered together in response to the arrest of a friend or relative, they are soon lined up behind the slogan 'Free the Leader.' They are transformed into constituents. The leaders cease to be isolated. They acquire a mass mase. From this initial community they move to other victims of repression, to swell their ranks. *The way to fight repression is to build a mass movement of support and legal defense for the 10 in jail or facing jail for contempt of court. Our responsibility in the immediate future is to increase our resistance and struggle--by any means necessary--against the government and the forces which dominate the country. We must do so in ways which will swell our ranks and broaden the support for all victims of repression, for the present movement is still too isolated.* The constituents initially united to support the victims of repression become shock troops of the movement, the army of the organization. The aspiring leader ceases to be an isolated individual and becomes the spokesman of a constituency, the leader of a mass base. The leader becomes the representative of all victims of repression, the interpreter of all resistance to repression. The leader becomes a historical force.

None of the weapons in the capitalist arsenal must be overlooked. All the manipulative techniques used by the ruling class to control the underlying population can, with skill, be used against the ruling class to create constituencies, to enhance the power of the revolutionary organization, to establish the power of the leader. For the aspiring leader, *that scenario is a whole interview in itself.* It involves *moving from strong local projects to regional structures to some kind of functional equivalent to a radical national party. The most difficult work is the organization of specific constituencies that can offer a community radical political education, power to combat effectively certain self-interest issues, a forum for people seeking new definitions for their lives and their work, and a method for relating the specific constituency to other parts of the movement. —Dare we visualize--and dare we build--a movement 10, 100, or 1000 times as great as the force we now represent? Dare we shirk this responsibility?* In a society of represented power, there is no reason for revolutionary leaders to shirk this responsibility. Although it is physically impossible for one individual to wield the powers of thousands, this is precisely what is possible with represented power. Although the self-powers of individuals cannot be concentrated in one individual, estranged powers can be concentrated. A single individual can speak for and decide for an entire community. Such power can be built by *using a service approach analogous to the style of the old political machines. If you have a problem--clothes, food, problems concerning the police, welfare, housing, employment and schools--you can come and get help.* The goal, of course, is *to build a militant united front against imperialism.* Whatever advances the bearers of anti-imperialist consciousness is a means to this goal. In the hands of the revolutionary leader, *the style of the old political machine,* and the electoral apparatus as well, become powerful instruments for shaping people into a mass base. The revolutionary leader cannot afford to reject the capitalist instruments for the establishment of represented power. The point is to use these instruments dialectically. *The first response, that of liberalism on first seeing social evils, is to participate in electoral activity to change society, to make reforms. Because all that is being sought is reform, there is no contradiction in electoral participation. The second level, however, corresponding to radicalism, by negation, where evils are seen in relation to one another, involves the refusal to participate in elections out of a recognition of the impossibility of reform. Radicalism does not yet say what is possible, however, and therefore rejects all possibilities. The third period of revolutionary consciousness involves, by further negation, participation in electoral struggle; first, because it can best be demonstrated to people that the process is futile, through the process itself; and second, that it is a useful forum and place where people gather and can be spoken to, and, since it is no longer believed in, it cannot compromise effectiveness. Where a radical sees the system's strength and totality one-dimensionally, the revolutionary sees its internal contradictions and weaknesses.*

As soon as leaders with revolutionary consciousness participate in electoral struggle, they will discover, through the process itself, that they can use the process even more fully *to gather together people who can be spoken to.* If they can establish a foothold in the electoral apparatus, they will discover that *we have to work for power, because this country does not function by morality, love and nonviolence, but by power. We are determined to win political power, with the idea of moving on from there into activity that would have economic effects. With power, the masses could make or participate in making the decisions which govern their destinies, and thus create basic change in their day-to-day lives. The right to vote has to be won. —All must be united so we can win political power and achieve self determination. —The colonies must be liberated. People must come together to elect representatives and to force those responsible to speak to their needs.* Leaders with a revolutionary ideology thus *begin to exert palpable pressure for a redistribution of resources.* They begin to exert palpable pressure on the federal government. *Who else but the federal government has the power to create jobs, to raise income, and to build the schools and hospitals and other civic centers required for the age of decency?* By these means a revolutionary organizer becomes an economic as well as a political force in the community. Further growth of the organization requires further growth of its economic power. To seize this economic power, revolutionary educators have to draft projects and proposals. *Here again, any community movement faces an educational task of major proportions: to pose clear and democratically supported models of new communities within the power of the Federal Government to support and fund. —Ultimately, the economic foundations of this country must be shaken. —Here again, any proposed solution must be national, and will require federal action. —The creation of a national party must come about. There must be reallocation of money.*

The political representation of the proletariat is only one of the functions of the revolutionary establishment. An even more important function is the education of the proletariat. As high school teachers and university professors, revolutionary leaders directly raise the consciousness of working people. They thus prepare people to accept the long term plans of the revolutionary organization; they create future followers. *One cannot overestimate the need for concrete alternatives to be presented to these ordinary people. Slogans ('let the people decide,' 'crush American imperialism') simply don't cut ice. We desperately need the development of short-range strategies and plans that both will foster greater radical consciousness and can be implemented; only this will shatter their cynicism. They must realize that change is possible before accepting our long-term plans. Why is it important for professional radicals to consider these people? Pragmatically, the reasons are very clear: They are the common people, and without at least their support we cannot build a democratic mass movement. However, there is another reason for activities such as teaching in community colleges. We can draw from their experience as well as asking them to accept our vision.* There is an even more important reason for professional radicals to consider these people, the proletarians. If they did not consider them, they would not be professional radicals but merely professional; they would not be revolutionary professors but merely professors; they would not serve the revolutionary establishment but the capitalist establishment. It is from this fate that the revolutionary ideology saves them. *Professors for Social Action becomes a framework of community. Nationally as well as locally PSA is an arena of toil for community of spirit and the continuing tribulations stimulate a community of salvation with other concerned human beings.* Without the revolutionary ideology, the Professors for Social Action would not be distinguishable from the staff members who serve industrial enterprises, the government or the military. Without the revolutionary ideology, revolutionary intellectuals would not be distinguishable from management consultants, government advisers, military researchers, professional advertisers, public relations men, or psychologists. With the ideology, they become important members of the revolutionary establishment. With revolutionary consciousness, they are able to confront the sophisticated data of their pro-imperialist colleagues with the sophisticated techniques of their fields. If the government offers to fund their researches, they do not refuse the funds, because they do not *see the system's strength and totality one-dimensionally; the revolutionary sees its internal contradictions and weaknesses.* Engagement in government-supported research makes the revolutionary professor a major figure in the revolutionary establishment. First of all, the academic credentials, the numerous published articles, the importance of the professor in the field, raise the prestige of the entire movement. Secondly, the revolutionary professor's substantial income sometimes becomes an important source of movement funds.

As for the revolutionary professor's research, *since it is no longer believed in, it cannot compromise effectiveness.* The ultimate purpose of the research is to serve the revolutionary vanguard in its struggle to seize State power. The findings are not interpreted from the standpoint of capitalist ideology, but from the standpoint of revolutionary ideology. Whether the subject is the Third World, the ghetto, agriculture or genetics, the ultimate conclusion is always the same: the indispensability of revolutionary leadership. This conclusion is also the premise. Therefore, if the research is currently usable only by the class in power, this is accidental and temporary. This is not the true purpose of the research. The problems it poses cannot ultimately be solved by the fragmented ruling class currently in power. They cannot ultimately be solved *until the triumph of the world socialist revolution,* until *the representatives of revolutionary proletarian internationalism succeed in taking power* over *all the working and exploited people of the world.* Only then will the partial and fragmented researches be synthesized into a universal and total ideology. Only then will the true purpose of the revolutionary research be realized: the destruction of the hegemony of capitalist

ideology over the minds of men and the establishment of the hegemony of revolutionary ideology. Only then will the revolutionary
intellectuals in the offices of the academic establishment collectively
personify the entire spiritual life of modern society.

Academic as well as non-academic professions offer aspiring
leaders numerous avenues to the establishment of power. *The Professions offer radicals an unusual diversity of opportunities, particularly
if radical action is seen as broader in scope than merely the gathering
of sufficient forces to overthrow the capitalist system in one cataclys-
mic operation. Four areas of action suggest themselves:*

*1. Organizing of services. The radical professional, along with
his counterparts in other fields, can serve an essential role as technical
consultant--*

*2. Work within academic institutions and professional organi-
zations--*

*3. Research, scholarship and public education. The mental
professional, in collaboration with social scientists of other disci-
plines, can make social change itself the target of his study--*

4. The practice of law. In a society where individuals are
atomized and the community is powerless, nothing stands between
the individual and the State—except the lawyer. The revolutionary
lawyer can serve the essential role of mediator between revolutionary
individuals and the capitalist State.

The most important avenue to power is the government itself.
Government posts provide the best vantage point for the materializa-
tion of the revolutionary ideology. The revolutionary ideology defines
the central crisis of modern capitalism. *The fundamental contradiction of capitalism between the social nature of production and the
private ownership of the means of production is revealed in the era
of monopoly capitalism as a monetary and fiscal crisis.* Only experts
who are informed by the revolutionary ideology, only revolutionary
experts, are able to deal with the fundamental contradiction, to
respond to the needs of the people. *Millions of people have come to
realize that they are ruled by a network of bureaucracies responding
not to the needs of the people they rule but to the needs of capital.*
There would be no monetary or fiscal crisis if people were ruled by a
network responding to the needs of the people they rule. There
would be no monetary or fiscal crisis in *a socialist society governed
by a dictatorship of the proletariat led by the Workers' Party which
follows a unitary ideology composed exclusively of the ideas of the
party secretary-general based on the creative application of Marxism-
Leninism to the conditions that obtain.* If revolutionary fiscal experts
creatively applied the ideas of the party secretary-general to the
fundamental contradiction, people would no longer be ruled by institutions that are separated from the people. The people's needs would
be fulfilled because the people would no longer be clients of the

ruling institutions; they would be constituents. *The unfulfilled needs of millions of people cannot be met by capital. Although many of the ruling institutions claim to be representative or in some way responsible to the people that they affect, in fact they are separated from the people. The people that are affected by them are clients and not constituents. The bureaucracies are independent of the people and follow the needs and logic of capital.*

There would be no fiscal crisis if workers controlled production through a democratic administration of the economy. The workers who controlled production through such an administration would realize that *Whatever we have, all we have built, is entirely owing to the correct leadership of comrade party secretary-general.* The consolidated power of the entire administration would regain its former grandeur. The office of the Leader would be experienced as a personal power because the Leader's ideas would form the basis for people's experience. The bureaucracies would no longer be independent of the people; they would no longer follow the needs and logic of Capital. They would follow the needs and logic of the ideology. *Ideology is the key to the revolution and socialist construction, and the Leader is the key to ideology. The leader founds and leads the party which is the vanguard of the working class and the general staff of the revolution. He is the supreme brain of the class and the heart of the party. He is the center of the unity and solidarity of the working class and the entire revolutionary masses. There is no center except him. It is an indispensable need in leading socialism and communism to a final triumph to resolutely defend the leader of the revolution and form a steel-like ring around him to strictly protect and carry out his revolutionary ideas.*

The historical experience of the revolutionary socialist movement has made it clear that the Dictatorship of the Proletariat consists of the absolute dictatorship of the leader of the proletariat. In conditions where this goal has not yet been realized, every increase in the power of a revolutionary leader is a step in the right direction. Every seizure of an available form of power is a revolutionary act. The establishment of available forms of power provides leaders experience in wielding forms of personified power. And the wielding of these forms of power requires the experience they've already acquired as leaders of the revolutionary organization. In short, available forms of power correspond perfectly with the experience as well as the aspirations of revolutionary leaders. The experience as well as the aspirations are solidly grounded in the social relations of the ruling system. In the language of classical revolutionary theory, neither the experience nor the aspirations are utopian. They are not based on the potential powers of individuals. They are grounded in the historically given powers of individuals. They are grounded in a historical situation where some are good at handling machines, others at handling abstractions; some at thinking, others at typing—a historical situation characterized by an efficient division between the labor of decision and the labor of execution. The experience which makes revolutionary leaders confident of their ability to deal with society's fundamental contradictions is not the experience of the producer but the experience of the official. By internalizing the powers of social offices, revolutionary leaders become personifications of social powers and cease to be mere individuals. The power to deal with the central contradiction does not reside in the individual revolutionary leader, but in the State office. The confidence of a revolutionary leader is not self-confidence in the individual's own powers. Such self-confidence is in fact rare among revolutionary leaders due to the fact that the self-powers, the creative abilities, of a leader are in general undeveloped; the failure to develop these powers is the form of the leader's sacrifice to the revolutionary goal. The confidence of the revolutionary leader is confidence in the ability to wield the powers of a State office. What the individual leader cannot do, the office can do. What no individual can do, the office of the central Leader can do. By internalizing the power of the Leader, individuals simultaneously internalize their own powerlessness. Every act which lies within the sphere of influence of the Leader is out of bounds for an individual. Individuals come to feel themselves unable to wield their own powers over the environment. The Leader can do everything. The individual can do nothing.

Unfortunately, even the seizure of available forms of power becomes difficult in conditions of developed productive forces. The wielding of these powers presupposes the prevalence of *people who cannot dispense with subordination, control and managers.* But the continuing development of society's productive forces eliminates the indispensability of *subordination, control and managers.* This phenomenon is understood by the theory of revolutionary consciousness. In the terminology of this theory, the less people are oppressed, the more they are privileged; the less their consciousness is revolutionary, the more it is bourgeois. The more the primitive accumulation of Capital is in the past, the less do people need social relations instrumental to the primitive accumulation of Capital. The more developed society's productive forces, the less do people need to be forced to develop productive forces. This phenomenon has the character of a historical law. In the language of the theory of consciousness it could be called the Law of Diminishing Revolutionary Consciousness. The law could be summarized as follows: the less people are deprived of the material consequences of *subordination, control and managers,* the less their need to subordinate themselves to the control of managers for the sake of these material consequences. Diminishing revolutionary consciousness creates a crisis for revolutionary leaders. This law is undoubtedly one of the factors that accounts for the failure of revolutionary leaders to establish a classical Dictatorship of the Proletariat over an industrially developed working class. Diminishing revolutionary consciousness is not the result of errors or shortcomings of revolutionary leaders. It is a result of the development of society's productive forces. The possibility of failure of revolutionary leaders is rooted In the contradiction between the historical level of development of the productive forces and the historical accomplishments of revolutionary organizations.

The historical accomplishment of revolutionary organizations has been to launch the primitive accumulation of Capital in regions where this development had been stunted. But the working classes of industrially developed regions already completed this historical task, under the leadership of an earlier form of revolutionary vanguard. The social relations created by Dictatorships of the Proletariat have been the modern State, developed commodity production and a sophisticated division of labor. But these are precisely the social relations that hamper and repress the further development of the industrial working class. In short, the possibility of the failure of modern socialism in the field where socialism originated—among industrial workers—is created by the historical development of socialism and of the industrial working class. At its origin socialism was a common ground, a means of discourse, for all individuals who alienate their productive activity. To the extent that slaves have a language distinct from the language of their masters, socialism was the language of those who simultaneously created and were enslaved by the State, commodity production and the division of labor. The historical accomplishment of successful revolutionary leaders has been to put the language of socialism at the service of the State, commodity production and the division of labor. This historical accomplishment makes it extremely difficult to re-introduce to the working class which had given birth to it, not socialism in its 19th century form of a struggle for the reappropriation of self-powers, but socialism in its historically successful form of an ideology of leadership. In conditions of developed productive forces, revolutionary leaders confront a working class which no longer needs the State, commodity production and the division of labor. It is to these workers that revolutionary leaders propose their program of State power, iron discipline and unquestioning obedience. And of course the leaders quickly discover that this *privileged* working class, this *aristocracy of labor,* this *bourgeois proletariat* has *deserted to the bourgeoisie.* These *prisoners of bourgeois ideology* do not embrace the revolutionary program as a daring and imaginative vision of the future; they regard it as a nightmare of the past.

In the perspective of modern revolutionary theory, the crisis of the developed proletariat is a crisis of leadership. The crisis does not reside in the extent to which workers capitulate to the prevailing conditions of production. The crisis resides in the extent to which their failure to capitulate dispenses with revolutionary organizations. The crisis resides in the fact that these workers move without the ideology, leadership and historical experience of the revolutionary vanguard. The ferment of this developed working class is not revolutionary because it lacks revolutionary consciousness; it does not take the form of mass conversion to the ideology of a revolutionary leader. It takes the form of acts rendered possible by the development of the productive forces, and a growing failure to perform acts rendered unnecessary by the level of development of the productive forces. The ferment takes the form of absenteeism, sabotage, wildcat strikes, occupations of productive plants, and even attempts to dismantle the entire social order. It takes the form of a growing resistance to State power, a growing refusal to alienate productive activity, a growing rejection of specialization. For aspiring leaders, the crisis resides in the fact that this ferment is not a response to revolutionary ideology or leadership, but to the historical level of development of society's productive forces.

The crisis of revolutionary leadership is a result of the major historical developments of this century. While revolutionary leaders were realizing their historical accomplishments, the working class that had been considered the gravedigger of capitalism continued to dig. While revolutionary rulers were adapting the language of this class to the needs of a State about to embark on the primitive accumulation of Capital, the working class continued to create the productive forces which eliminated the need for the social relations of Capital accumulation. While revolutionary leaders continued to enlarge the sphere of State power, the working class continued to remove the historical basis of State power. As a result, the one-time vehicle for the accumulation of Capital has played out its historic role. The social relations which once lubricated the development of society's productive forces enter their period of decline. Their sole historic role becomes to reproduce themselves, a role which they increasingly perform by hampering the further development of the productive forces. The once-dynamic agents of electrification, mechanization, industrialization become a historical anomaly. The accelerated transformation of all the material conditions of life slows down to the point when mainly the names of the dynasties and the dates of the wars change. The Age of Progress flattens out into an Egyptian millennium. The lubricant turns to sand. The one-time agent becomes a fetter.

The Pharaonic dynasties declined for three thousand years. But aspiring leaders should not interpret this fact with unwarranted optimism. It does not mean that the social conditions required for the establishment of revolutionary leadership will continue to be available for three thousand years. Unlike the Pharaonic dynasties, the ruling classes of the period of Capital accumulation sit on a dynamo which their own historical activity brought into being. This dynamo constantly threatens to cut short their period of decline. The dynamo consists of individuals who are in daily contact with the constantly changing productive forces; individuals who are expected to be simultaneously automatic and imaginative, simultaneously obedient and creative. Unlike aspiring Pharaohs, aspiring modern leaders cannot count on these workers to continue to alienate their productive powers to Capital and their power of community to the State for the next 3000 years. The duration of the Egyptian decline is only one historical instance; it does not provide a basis for certainty. Frozen history, death in life, may only be the mask of modern society, and not its real face. The mask is all that is visible because the vision of the ruling class is in every epoch the ruling vision. But there are unmistakable signs of ferment and agitation just below the still mask. Unlike the peasants of ancient Egypt, modern workers have much to gain from the appropriation of society's productive forces.

The historical consequences of the Dictatorship of the Proletariat can only be realized in conditions where these consequences have not yet been realized. This is why the seizure of State power has succeeded mainly among people who had been deprived of the dominant historical reality of the capitalist epoch. This is why the ideology of the Dictatorship of the Proletariat, of growth rates of national income, of the new Socialist Man, has appealed only to *people in countries oppressed by imperialism.* The ideology was accepted because it was understood to refer to the modern State, commodity production and the division of labor. The rule of the vanguard party was not understood as an end in itself but as a means toward the full realization of the dominant historical reality of the capitalist epoch. The revolutionary organization offered people deprived of the amenities of modern social life the prospect of becoming professors, factory managers and policemen.

However, in conditions where the material consequences of capitalist social relations have already been realized, revolutionary leaders with portfolios to State offices have been hard put to point to any material consequences of their victory other than their rule. The less people need social relations instrumental to the accumulation of Capital, the more must leaders create a consciousness which regards the seizure of State power by revolutionary leaders as a good in itself. In such conditions it becomes a major feat for revolutionary leaders to maintain the conviction that the conscious vanguard of the proletariat performs a critical service for the proletariat. This conviction can no longer be implanted in the proletariat itself, because of the erosive effects of the law of diminishing consciousness. This conviction nevertheless remains the cornerstone of the revolutionary ideology, since without it aspiring leaders would never subject themselves to the years of self-deprivation, to the sacrifice of desires and abilities, which their revolutionary profession demands. Without this conviction, the unquestioning devotion required by the ideology and the faithful service required by the organization would not be endured. But the conviction can no longer be communicated; one must neither lose it nor spread it; one must learn to keep it to oneself. A revolutionary leader who explicitly presented himself as the culmination, the apex, and the sole consequence of the proletariat's struggle for socialism, would not thereby increase his stature. In conditions of developed productive forces, the revolutionary ideology cannot be made to refer to any material consequences or historical social relations, because these consequences and relations are already past necessities and present fetters. The terms of the ideology must be made to refer only to other terms of the ideology: Revolution means Socialism, Socialism means Power, Power means Revolution. The terms of the ideology must be presented as abstract truths, as parts of the Idea. Only then can the coup of a *Left-Leaning General* be presented as a victory of the *workers' movement*. The *General* is no longer to be considered the representative, or even the consciousness, of the *workers' movement*. The *General* believes in the IDEA of the *workers' movement,* and the General's coup is therefore the victory of the IDEA. Thus it becomes possible for the idea of the workers' movement to seize State power without the workers themselves moving. In fact, this becomes the last possibility for revolutionary leaders in conditions where the workers will not move within the path historically experienced by the world socialist movement, the path to the seizure of State power. In such conditions, the independent movement of the working class, no matter how broad its sweep, no longer has interest for revolutionary leaders except as an illustration of failure. Such independent movement fails before it begins because the *independence* is above all independence from the idea of the seizure of State power, the central idea and experience of the world socialist movement. The Idea cannot be victorious if those struggling do not believe in it.

Revolutionary leaders who seize power in conditions of developed productive forces have to emphasize solely the *idea* of socialism, because in such conditions the seizure of State power can have no material consequences other than the rule of the idea. In order to lay the ground for the seizure of State power in conditions of developed productive forces, revolutionary organizers have to raise the consciousness of the revolutionary masses to a recognition of the Leader as the carrier of the Idea. If it was already true in *countries oppressed by imperialism,* it is even more true in countries not oppressed by imperialism that *Ideology is the key to revolution and socialist construction* and that *the Leader is key to ideology.* The consciousness of an already industrialized proletariat cannot be stimulated by the example of an industrialized nation. It has to be raised to an acceptance of the thought of the Leader *per se.* To an even greater extent than any people in countries oppressed by imperialism, working people who themselves create contemporary productive forces are made to accept the revolutionary proposition that *Whatever we have, all we have built, is entirely owing to the correct leadership of the Leader.* This consciousness is raised by propaganda before the revolution, and by more powerful means after the seizure of State power. Universal acceptance of this proposition is equivalent to National Liberation. Revolutionary leaders who successfully seized State power in conditions of developed productive forces were the first to define the key struggle of the contemporary era as the struggle for national liberation. National liberation is the only form of liberation that can be realized by means of the seizure of State power. It was also these revolutionary leaders who first defined the fundamental contradiction of modern capitalism as the conflict between oppressed and oppressor nations. This is the only contradiction of modern capitalism that is resolved as soon as a revolutionary leader seizes the State apparatus.

In conditions of developed productive forces, the material consequences of the seizure of State power in *countries oppressed by imperialism* have to be simulated. The key historical accomplishment of the world socialist movement, the primitive accumulation of Capital, does not have a real context in conditions where primitive accumulation has already been carried out. This context has to be ideologically created. It is the function of revolutionary nationalist ideology to create the context for a second primitive accumulation of Capital. *The question of fundamental importance to the revolution is: Who are our friends and who are our enemies?* Oppressor nations, namely inhabitants of other countries, are the enemy, and therefore the source of primitive accumulation. Once the nation's enemies are defined, the question of fundamental importance is answered and the revolutionary program is launched. At this point it becomes necessary for revolutionary leaders to abandon the pacifism of the industrial working class whose socialist language is still being borrowed. Wars of national liberation are the sole means to national liberation. War is the only efficient instrument for liberation from oppressor nations. War is the only effective way to transform the inhabitants of other countries into sources of primitive accumulation. Consequently, the central institution required for the realization of national liberation is the national liberation army. The comradeship of those who kill together and the solidarity of those who die together replace the flabby petit-bourgeois pacifism of the industrial proletariat. A morality based on iron discipline, unquestioning obedience and boundless sacrifice

118

replaces the *petty bourgeois atmosphere which permeates and corrupts the proletariat and causes constant relapses among the proletariat into petty-bourgeois spinelessness, disunity, individualism, and alternate moods of exaltation and dejection. The strictest centralization and discipline are required within the political party of the proletariat in order to counteract this. Without an iron party tempered in the struggle, without a party capable of watching and influencing the mood of the masses, it is impossible to conduct such a struggle successfully.* The construction of a large proletarian army and a powerful socialist police, the waging of a permanent war of national liberation, and the liquidation of countless counter-revolutionaries who did not serve the people, have been the key historical accomplishments of revolutionary socialist nationalism in power. However, the seizures of power in conditions of developed productive forces have not made the repetition of this feat easier for modern revolutionary leaders. They have not counteracted the erosive effects of the law of diminishing revolutionary consciousness.

None of the forms of conscious revolutionary activity devised so far seem able to counteract the effects of the law of diminishing consciousness. In its ferment, the developed proletariat deprives itself of the direction provided by revolutionary leadership, it dispenses with the discipline provided by revolutionary organizations, and it lacks the consciousness provided by revolutionary ideology. Because of this lack of guidance, the developed proletariat fails to distinguish between its imperialist enemies and its anti-imperialist friends. If it is hostile to the discipline of capitalist production, it is equally hostile to the labor discipline required for the Construction of Socialism. If it is hostile to the authority of the capitalist State, it is equally hostile to the authority of the Socialist State. This undirected proletariat struts indifferently across the distinctions provided by revolutionary consciousness. When it takes steps to abolish capitalist commodity production, it increasingly turns first of all against its own conscious vanguard. Aspiring revolutionary leaders are left no choice but to define this proletariat as privileged, bourgeois, aristocratic, and therefore in its essence counter-revolutionary. The gulf between the developed proletariat and its conscious vanguard continues to widen. The more extensive and well known the historical accomplishments of revolutionary vanguards, the more the spontaneous activity of the proletariat is anarchic, carnivalous, undisciplined and undirected. Not only does the proletariat become increasingly deprived of the guidance of revolutionary leadership; the revolutionary vanguard becomes increasingly isolated from the proletariat. Those who respond to the social possibilities of the contemporary productive forces are not drawn to revolutionary organizations. Those who are drawn to revolutionary organizations are not drawn there by the possibilities of the productive forces. The two seem to stand on opposite sides of a historical watershed. They almost seem to live in different epochs. Where the one sees the possibility for enjoyment the other sees the necessity for sacrifice. Where the one sees the chance for play the other sees the need for discipline. Where the one experiments with the unknown, the other applies the tried and tested. Where the one develops self-powers, the other develops estranged powers. Where the one looks forward toward *the self government of the producers, creating a democracy on their own, in their own way,* the other looks backward toward *a socialist society governed by a dictatorship of the proletariat led by the Workers' Party which follows a unitary ideology composed exclusively of the ideas of the Leader.*

The organizations of the left become the last refuge for those who seek order, discipline, coherent ideology, and guidance. Only the organizations of the left are able to provide understanding in an increasingly anarchic situation. Only the organizations of the left are able to make sense out of a growing chaos. *Ideology is the key.* The organizations of the left become the last refuge for those who would be lost without the conviction that *in modern civilized countries classes are led by political parties; that political parties are directed by more or less stable groups composed of the most authoritative, influential and experienced members who are elected to the most responsible positions and are called leaders. —The leader founds and leads the party which is the vanguard of the working class and the general staff of the revolution. He is the supreme brain of the class and the heart of the party. He is the center of the working class. There is no center except him. —All this is elementary. All this is simple and clear. Why replace this by some rigmarole?* Instead of replacing all this by some rigmarole, it is necessary to *form a steel-like ring around the leader to strictly protect and carry out his revolutionary ideas.* It is necessary to protect and nourish every head in which the thought of the leader takes root. Only by such means can the organizations of the left continue to serve the revolution, serve history, and serve the people. Activity which nourishes and spreads the thought of the leader lays the foundation for a truly representative democracy in which each individual is able to participate in at least a fragment of the power personified by the leader. In a pre-revolutionary situation, such activity could take the form of selling the thoughts of leaders for a small profit margin. This would make the revolutionary ideology available at low prices, and at the same time would provide an income for the revolutionary organizers spreading the ideology. The path to the seizure of State power would then be paved by small entrepreneurs. In a period of agitation and ferment such activity serves the people and responds directly to their needs. The ferment itself provides inspirations for products as well as a market for revolutionary ideas. If the ferment becomes an ongoing and normal part of daily life, the revolutionary entrepreneurs could easily establish powerful and influential institutions devoted to the *unitary ideology composed exclusively of the ideas of the Leader.* But if the ferment becomes independent activity, or if it subsides, the revolutionary organizers are likely to become discouraged with the minuteness of the accomplishment compared to the greatness of the task.

120

In a situation where *the historical experience of the revolutionary socialist movement* is not what anyone wants, serving the people revolutionary ideology and leadership is not a small task. It is a Gargantuan enterprise. It requires force as well as propaganda. The task of knocking capitalist ideas out of people's heads requires a propaganda apparatus larger than the capitalist academic community and more efficient than the capitalist advertising industry. It requires security measures which cut off counter-revolutionary anti-leadership ideas before they spread. The question of fundamental importance to revolutionary leaders is not only to define the real friends and the real enemies, but also to weed out the real enemies. Defining the real enemies is the function of the revolutionary ideology. Weeding them out is the function of guardians of the revolutionary ideology. The real enemies of revolutionary vanguards are powerful and widespread. They spread with the continuing development of the productive forces. They are in every plant, in every office, in every neighborhood. Revolutionary guardians confront them in every meeting of every group. The real enemies of revolutionary vanguards are independent workers. Their independence, their rejection of revolutionary leadership, sows the seeds of anarchy. Their rejection of revolutionary discipline creates chaos in every office and department of the revolutionary establishment. *Their demands are not new to the guardians. A number of previous workers had also called for general undifferentiation of job function, abolition of serious professional technical work, the abolition of the political probation period prior to becoming a voting member of the staff, the abolition of centralized direction of production. Some have wanted to abolish any form of leadership, or 'hierarchy' in their terms, altogether. The guardians have discussed these and similar demands, usually grouped by their advocates under the rubric of 'workers' control and internal democracy,' and have democratically--at times unanimously, rejected them.* The real enemies of the revolutionary vanguard are all those who reject the modern State, universal commodity production and the progressive division of labor. They are contemporary producers who reject capitalist supervision, control and managers. Their opposition to the historical accomplishments of capitalism is not new. Producers struggled against the constraints of capitalism during its entire development. In fact, craftsmen, artisans and peasants resisted the very rise of capitalism. Thus revolutionary guardians classify the contemporary enemies of capitalism together with all historical opponents of capitalism, and define the contemporary producers as *petit-bourgeois craftsmen, artisans and peasants.* The task of modern revolutionary ideology is to identify all opposition to capitalism with pre-capitalist opposition to capitalism. From the standpoint of pre-capitalist social forms, capitalism is progressive, and all opposition to it is *reactionary, petit-bourgeois, anarcho-syndicalist, and petty capitalist* at the same time. The real enemies of the revolutionary vanguard are all the present and past enemies of capitalism. The real potential for human liberation, the revolutionary vision of the future, is found by looking to capitalism. The task of the revolutionary guardians, who are today known as Marxist-Leninists or simply as Marxists, is to weed out *the political ideas of workers' self-management and control, decentralism and local autonomy, opposition to the division of labor and all forms of hierarchy. Their expression has been an undercurrent within and without working class and socialist movements from the beginnings 150 to 200 years ago, but were particularly widespread, in a variety of forms, during the earlier stages of capitalist development. This is the clue to the class character of these trends, which Marxists have described as the reaction of petit-bourgeois craftsmen, artisans and peasants to the reorganization and growth of manufacturing at the beginning of the indsutrial revolution. In this sense, the demand for 'workers' control' or 'self-management' of this or that factory or workshop meant, in essence, 'give us back the ownership of our tools.' The demand for 'local autonomy' meant a return to the exclusiveness of the guilds or the self-contained isolation of the rural village. Opposition to the division of labor implied a return to the equality of the guilds where each individual did similar but separate work. Combined with this was the opposition to all hierarchies, a reaction to the social organization and supervision in the individual factory. As for the state, the attitude was similar to that of all petty capitalists: the less of it--and its taxes and trade regulations--the better. This hankering for the return of the old order now superceded by modern industry is why Marxists use the terms 'reactionary' and 'petit-bourgeois' to characterize anarcho-syndicalism. The real potential for human liberation is found by looking to the future, not the past.* The past only contains *reactionary and petit-bourgeois* opposition to capitalism, whereas what the future holds in store is liberation in the form of the modern State, universal commodity production, the progressive division of labor, all forms of hierarchy, and the prevailing contemporary forms of supervision, control and managers.

All the living individuals who refuse to subordinate themselves, and all the past individuals who refused to subordinate themselves to the dominant social authorities of the capitalist epoch are the real enemies of the Party of the Proletariat, and therefore, since the language of socialism is still being borrowed, they are all agents of the bourgeoisie. *Whoever weakens ever so little the iron discipline of the party of the proletariat (especially during the time of its dictatorship) actually aids the bourgeoisie against the proletariat. —Within the party, there must be no one lagging behind when an order is given by the leadership to 'march forward,' no one turning right when the order is 'left.' —The strictest centralization and discipline are required within the political party of the proletariat in order to counteract this.* In order to weed the real enemies of the proletariat out of the organization, in order to be sure that no one is lagging behind when an order is given by the leader, a political probation period needs to be instituted. Only after this probation period can an aspiring leader become a member of the staff. If this probation period is to be at all effective, revolutionary organizations need to equip themselves with modern instruments for measuring the iron discipline and unquestioning obedience of an applicant. In order to administer the probation, it is necessary to strap the aspiring member to an appropriately wired chair. The leader administers the probation from another room. The leader reads a question into a microphone and hears the aspirant's answer over a speaker. In response to the appropriate question, the aspirant must answer *Ideology is the key to revolution and socialist construction.* The answer cannot merely contain this thought. It must be stated in these words. Any alteration in the phrasing is an indication of *petit bourgeois individualism. —To deviate from socialist ideology in the slightest degree means strengthening bourgeois ideology.* All this is elementary. When the correct answer is *The Leader is key to ideology,* the aspirant deviates fatally by using 'Dictator' or 'Ruler' in the place of 'Leader.' In front of the probator is a panel of buttons. Labels identify the amount of voltage administered to the aspirant by each button. The panel goes as high as 450 volts, and buttons corresponding to the highest voltages are marked 'caution, severe pain.' These higher voltages are only applied on *petit-bourgeois individualists* who refuse to answer *Whatever we have, all we have built, is entirely owing to the correct leadership of the Leader.* Only individuals who answer this question correctly are able to become instruments or media through whom the powers of the leader can be exercised. The office of the leader becomes legitimate only when the authority of the office and its occupant is internalized by all staff members. Only individuals who accept the legitimacy of the office can become voting members of the staff.

Unfortunately, even the strictest political probation period may fail to weed out the real enemies of the revolutionary organization. Individuals who accepted the thought of the leader during the probation period may deviate from it later. To be sure that no one deviates in the slightest degree, it might be necessary to keep the organization's membership down to five or six members. If the members of a small, closed vanguard do not engage in any practical activity, they can keep constant watch on each other. Furthermore, a miniature International whose members engage exclusively in thought can achieve the coherence required to embrace the entire world revolutionary movement. The basis for membership in such a revolutionary organization would be to appropriate, commit to memory, and on suitable occasions proclaim the thought of the most coherent member. If the appropriation of the coherence of the critique is the basis for membership, the miniature International is able to re-enact the great historical moments of the large Internationals. If the members learn to regard their membership as the only alternative to historical oblivion, all the powers of the great parties of the proletariat can be wielded on a very small scale. Even the Dictatorship of the Proletariat can be re-enacted in miniature, with purges of the incoherent, public confessions of errors, recantations of critiques of the critique, generous reinstatements, and even occasional mass expulsions of two or three members.

But if the organization consists of more than six members, and aspires to grow even larger, nothing can prevent the proliferation of enemies of revolutionary leadership short of a powerful and efficient security apparatus. In favorable circumstances this apparatus would take the form of a militia, a secret police, an army, or preferably all three combined. But we have seen that in conditions of developed productive forces, circumstances are not so favorable. Consequently other alternatives must be found. Revolutionary leaders of other countries command large liberation armies. Organizers can implant anti-imperialist consciousness among the workers by offering them the prospect of invasion from abroad. The people must be served, one way or the other. The historical situation does not leave room for flabby and sentimental alternatives. The central task of revolutionary leaders in conditions of developed productive forces is to liquidate the enemies of the proletariat's leaders. To this end, leaders must concentrate their attention on problems of security.

If revolutionary leaders are unable to serve the people with their own security forces, they will have no choice but to turn to the available security forces. There may be no other way to deal with *the petit-bourgeois atmosphere that encircles the proletariat on every side. The strictest centralization and discipline are required in order to counteract this.* The required centralization and discipline are such that only the armed forces are really adequate for the task. *While modern capitalism is highly organized within a given factory or industry, the relations between capitalists are characterized by the social anarchy of production. With the possible exception of the armed forces and some public utilities, the imperialist economy and state are neither centralized nor planned.* Those presently in control of the State apparatus do not adequately perform the specific office of the State, which is to use all available means to ensure that the power of community remains estranged. They perform this function only inside the walls of factories, in some public utilities and in the armed forces. The aim of revolutionary leaders is to extend centralization and planning to the society at large, to merge the estranged power of producers with the estranged power of community. Only then would the State directly determine the shape of the environment in which human beings live and the activities in which they engage. This is why *the working class must win political power by smashing the imperialist bureaucratized state apparatus, establish the social ownership of the productive forces and carry out centralized planning with a vengeance through a new state of its own based on the armed power of the people.* The armed power of the people, namely the armed forces, will of course remain intact since they were already adequately disciplined and centralized before the working class smashed and seized the State apparatus. In the meantime, in order to protect the revolutionary establishment at this late historical hour, revolutionary leaders would be well advised to turn to the last available instruments which can serve their ends: the armed forces and the police. Military power is the key to revolution and socialist construction in a situation where every attempt of individuals to realize their self-powers to the level made possible by contemporary productive forces is a threat to the existence of the entire revolutionary establishment. A revolutionary leader *should therefore have no other aim or thought, nor take up any other thing for his study, but war and its organization and discipline, for that is the only art that is necessary to one who commands. The chief cause of the loss of states is the contempt for this art. He ought, therefore, never to let his thoughts stray from the exercise of war; and in peace he ought to practice it more than in war, which he can do in two ways: by action and by study. As to exercise for the mind,* the revolutionary leader *ought to read history and study the actions of eminent men, see how they acted in warfare, examine the causes of their victories and defeats in order to imitate the former and avoid the latter.* Only by such means can the historical experience of the revolutionary socialist movement continue to spread across the world.

The Sources of M. Velli's Thought

M. Velli's Thought is a synthesis of the ideas of the major revolutionary leaders of the age. These ideas are printed in italics in the preceding text. The sources of these quotations are available for two letter stamps or two International Reply Coupons from AK Press, 3 Balmoral Place, Stirling, FK8 2RD, Britain.